Hinged

Clay Bracelets

new ways to link polymer clay bracelet parts

Gloria Uhler

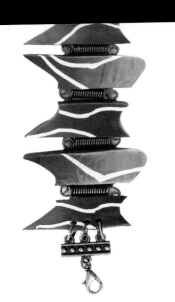
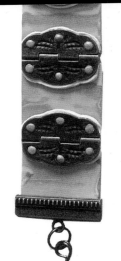

THE WORLD OF POLYMER CLAY ARTISTRY

These fortunes are yellowing with age but I keep them as reminders of my good fortune to have wandered into the world of polymer clay. It's like no craft environment I've ever been a part of. Inspiring and artistic, this world is filled with talented people.

Clay guilds exist all over the world just waiting for you to join. Members are generous with their time and expertise and many Guild groups pose challenges each month for their members; a project to create and present at a future meeting. You can't put a price on exchanging ideas and your creations with others in an environment where there is no judgment and no agenda.

Many Guilds have "clay days", a monthly gathering to work on personal projects, share expertise and occasionally get a visit from celebrity artists willing to talk about new techniques and tools.

In California, the San Diego and Orange County Guilds come together annually, along with clay artists from all over the country for four days of hands-on clay making, classes, and socializing. The event is called Sandy Camp, the brain child of Syndee Holt, well known artist, photographer and author in the Polymer Clay Community. Visit sdpcg.com for information.

Consider joining a Polymer Clay Guild in your area. A new hobby may be in store for you and I guarantee you'll meet a new friend!

ISBN 978-0-692-61332-0

Conceived, designed and produced by Gloria Uhler.

Photography by the author.

The projects in *Hinged Clay Bracelets* are copyrighted.
Instructions are intended for your personal use and may not be
taught or sold without permission.

The covers and interior contents of this book were created with
Silhouette Design software.

Please follow manufacturer's health and safety instructions.
Never use clay tools in conjunction with food intended for
consumption.

Acknowledgments

Heaps of gratitude go out to....

My husband; my technical advisor, math expert, engineer and my own personal Mr. Science who could tell
me a bracelet link wouldn't work before the concept was even executed. You have my appreciation for all
that and for always stepping up and keeping things running when I was preoccupied with clay.

Vicky, my oldest and dearest friend, who along with my newest friend Deborah, are sticklers for details and
helped me proof these pages.

The talented members of the Orange County Polymer Clay Guild who so kindly and patiently offered their
expertise. But especially to Donna and her big heart who always had answers when I needed them, or tools
to borrow, and who so generously offered the Orange County Guild members a monthly venue for coming
together.

Iris and Polyform Products for unflagging encouragement, friendship, and clay.

The San Diego Polymer Clay Guild who treated me like a member even when I wasn't. And for everyone at
Sandy Camp for giving me more to look forward to each October than Halloween.

HINGE (hǐnj) n. 1. a. A jointed or flexible device that allows the turning or pivoting of a part, such as a door or lid, on a stationary frame.

The word "hinged" in this book's title covers a lot of ground because on these pages you'll not only find actual hinges, but as promised, other fresh ideas for linking polymer clay bracelet parts. The solutions include chain, jump rings, wire, hardware hinges, spring hinges, clay, cord, magnets, and yes, clay! I've even shared my ideas on better bangles, what I call "bikini bangles", which are two piece versions of the traditional bracelet. Mine result in a better fit. New stretchy bracelet concepts and cuff wraps round out my collection of designs created exclusively for the clay medium. I hope you'll find inspiration in this book and most importantly, that you will have fun experimenting with these tutorials.

gloria

INTRODUCTION

Polymer clay is nothing short of magic and using it to create bracelets opens the door to unlimited design, texture and color possibilities. While the clay medium is freeing and visually limitless, the one daunting challenge in this wide array of creative possibilities has always been structure. It is the main reason there are so many similar cuff, bangle and simple stretchy clay bracelets being produced by designers today. You can easily connect clay parts for earrings and other projects but how do you get clay to conform around the wrist in new ways? You will find the answer here.

The bracelet tutorials in this book will take you off the beaten path and introduce you to unique polymer clay bracelet links that employ unexpected materials, designs, and tools.

You will learn how to create personalized bracelet forms and discover ways to produce bead textures and images with my stencil and stamping techniques.

If you own a stencil machine or have ever thought of purchasing one, you will be excited to know how it can broaden your clay making abilities. Read about that in these pages too.

You are on your way to bringing your imaginative concepts to fruition with flexible, and most importantly, wearable polymer clay creations. Novices as well as seasoned clay makers can benefit from this book. Just browse the photos and steps that will guide you to completing 25 clay bracelets using fresh concepts for structure.

Contents

THINGS TO REMEMBER

Repetition is boring and the pages of a book are valuable real estate. So here are things you will not be reminded of repeatedly in this book:

• Because most projects will require a pasta machine, tissue blades, craft knife, acrylic roller, jewelry pliers and cutters, these items will not be included in supply lists.

• Always condition clay before working on your project.

• Sanding is done in this order with wet/dry sandpaper - 400, 600, 800 and 1000 grit. Follow with buffing either by hand with a soft cloth or a rotary tool with a cloth attachment.

• When applying glaze, my choice is always *Future Floor Polish*. Research the Internet to find other good alternatives.

• When applying texture sheets or rubber stamps, mist the sheet with water or sprinkle it with baby powder to prevent it from sticking to the clay.

• Follow manufacturer's suggested time and temperature for curing clay. Always allow the clay to cool completely before handling.

• Allow glues and adhesives to set before proceeding to the next step.

• IMPORTANT! The settings on my conditioning machine range from one (thickest) through nine (thinnest). Your machine may differ.

• Work on bakers plastic or parchment paper whenever possible. It will allow you to turn your work easily when cutting with a craft knife and also make it convenient to lift the clay from the surface. Parchment is especially ideal for curing pieces and for wrapping around clay to hold things together during the curing process.

• Create rounded clay edges when using cutters by laying a sheet of bakers plastic on the clay first.

• When using top mounted hardware hinges, allow movement of thick clay bracelet pieces by beveling the vertical edges on the back side. In general, beads that will be separated by metal hinges may need to be beveled on the underside so that when the hinge is flexed, the bead edges do not bump against each other. This would prevent flexibility of the bracelet sections.

• "General Blending" throughout this book refers to rolling different colors of conditioned clay into tubes with your hands, twisting them together, flattening, rolling again, and folding in half. Repeat this process two or three times depending on the degree of blend you desire. When you think you have achieved it, sheet it on the pasta machine.

• I often refer to "scrap clay". There really is no such thing because most clay left over from other projects can be blended with new clay to create a fresh and exciting color.

WHAT TO EXPECT

Because this book focuses on the idea of connecting clay pieces for bracelets with various methods, you will not find elaborate explanations of artistic effects, color theory, or imprint technique. If you are unfamiliar with these subjects, you will find them fully explained in other books written by outstanding clay artists. Some of my recommendations are:
• *The Polymer Clay Artist's Guide* by Marie Segal
• *Patterns in Polymer* by Julie Picarello
• *Color Inspirations* by Lindly Haunani and Maggie Maggio

Techniques used in this book are noted on each page. They include:
• Mokumé Gané
• Sutton Slice
• Skinner Blend
• Canes
• Paper Stencils
• General Blending
• Templates
• Texture Sheets and Stamps

At the top of each tutorial page, I have listed important information you may want to find at a glance . This includes the type of connection linking bracelet parts (wire, cord, hinges, etc.), the technique, if a template was used, and bracelet size. Look to the bottom of the page to find clay colors used and supplies needed for the project.

Gold Wire Lifesavers

Wire • Mold • Skinner Blend • General Blend • Bracelet Me...

1. Prepare the Fuchsia and Yellow skinner blend and a Spanish Olive and White blend. Cut the clay blends into 3" squares. Stack all the squares and use a general blend technique to mix the colors.

2. Mist the medium cabochon mold. Press the clay into the mold. Slice away excess with a tissue blade positioned almost perpendicular to the mold. Save the colorful scraps for another project.

3. Pop the cl... a total of se... beads.

4. Sand and buff the clay to a sheen. If you are using a rotary tool, secure the bead with a pipe cleaner you can hold onto to prevent it from sailing across the room.

5. Cut six pieces of wire to measure two inches. Cut another to measure one inch. Slip a two inch wire into a bead. Curl the end just slightly to the center of the wire. Slip the other wire end into the next bead.

6. Curve the wires to cross in the center. Do not press them flat. Allow 1/2" between beads for movement. Trim both wires in the center with a 1/8" space between them.

1/2"

SUPPLIES

Premo
Fuchsia
Yellow
Spanish Olive
White
Cabochon Mold

Gold wire 16 - 18
Jewelry Glue
Crimp B...

BARE MINIMUM TOOLS

When I began working with polymer clay, my only tools were a craft knife and an acrylic roller. I was able to accomplish quite a bit with my meager implements. It was not long, however, before I realized how far I might go with an extended selection of gadgets that would make the work easier and the product more polished.

I mention this because many crafters new to polymer clay can be discouraged when they see craft books filled with extensive lists of tools that seem absolutely necessary. Quite honestly, if you cannot afford dedicated tools it is possible to still have fun with clay and produce satisfying projects. Many tools in this book may be substituted with items you find around the house or in the garage. One of the most replaceable tools is the rubber stamp or texture sheet. I will explain how to save money by creating your own on page 13.

After working with polymer clay for a time you will find yourself viewing your surroundings with a different eye. Suddenly a paper doily, puffy shelf liner, or a piece of lace will become a valuable tool for imprinting the surface of a clay creation.

Consider the objectives you want to accomplish, no matter what the project, and it will become clear which bare minimum tools are necessary. When you are creating bracelets, every piece of polymer clay must be manipulated in two ways: conditioned or rolled, and cut to a specific size or shape. Ideally there will be a third way - characterizing; creating texture, piercing, or altering the surface to add interest. With these three objectives in mind, rewarding projects can be created using tools you already have on hand.

BASIC TOOLS USED IN THIS BOOK

acrylic roller

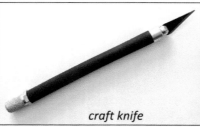
craft knife

bakers plastic

jewelry pliers & cutters

sculpting tools

tissue blades

pasta machine

sand paper

FUNDAMENTALS

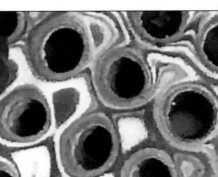

PERSONALIZED TEXTURE SHEETS AND STAMPS

A Money Saving Idea

Rubber stamps and texture sheets are part of every clay artist's tool box. They are important because detailed impressions are desirable on bead surfaces and add yet another element to the overall design.

I make many of my texture sheets and stamps and you can too. You do not have to have extensive artistic skills to create them in styles and sizes that suit your project. The very good news is that you can make them for pennies. A craft knife or stencil cutting machine, card stock, adhesive and polymer clay is all you need.

Positive and negative images can be created with the same basic design to form both raised (texture sheet) and depressed (stamp) images on your clay.

The first step in creating your own texture sheets and stamps is to search online at Google for an image. Using the word "stencil" in the search will return line drawing type images perfect for your purpose.

1 - Size the image and print three copies onto card stock. Use a craft knife to cut out the image or let your stencil cutting machine do the work.

3 - If you have chosen an intricate design, cutting with a craft knife might seem a bit daunting but keep in mind your finished piece can be reused several times. Be sure all the cut lines match up, then use spray adhesive or a glue stick to join the three stencils you have created. Also check that the cut openings match.

4 - Roll out scrap clay larger than your image on the conditioning machine's #1 setting.

5 - Powder the wrong side of your stencil and place it on the clay. Roll across it until the clay raises to the surface of the paper. Remove the stencil.

Three layers of card stock will result in a very satisfactory impression but you can use more layers if you like. Once the clay has cooled after curing, use it as you would any rubber stamp. To create more of a stamp-like surface, cut around the raw clay edges with a craft knife before curing.

6 - To create texture sheets, glue your card stock, die cut images together as you did for the stencils.

7 - Place your combined piece on the clay and roll across it. Remove the card stock from the clay.

8 - Cure the clay. Once the clay is cool, you can use it as you would any texture sheet.

BRACELET SIZING

It's All About The Math - The Simple Formula

The beauty of working with clay is that we have the option to create bracelets in any size we want. Designing your own does involve some math but it is not calculus or trigonometry. The measurements for beaded bracelets generally center around the width of each clay piece. The length of the pieces are optional.

While creating a bracelet, you will always be dealing with the same numbers if the bracelet is made for you. Keep in mind the average bracelet size is about 7 1/2". So let us assume for this explanation, that 7 1/2" is your ideal finished bracelet size. To determine the size of your clay pieces, the first thing you need to know is the clasp space. This number is different than the clasp size because the way in which the clasp connects to the beads will add to the clasp space. The clasp space is the number of inches between the last beads on each end of the strand, no matter what type of clasp you use. Subtract that number from 7 1/2". This result is the number of inches you have to work with to plan the size of your beads.

Let us further assume your clasp space is 1 1/2". Subtract that from the bracelet size of 7 1/2" and your beads would add up to 6" if they were butted together. There will inevitably be a space between each bead. Those spaces should be subtracted from 6". This will result in your final magic number. With it, anything is possible. You can create almost any width bead you like as long as the combined beads and their spaces do not exceed that magic number. If you prefer larger beads use fewer pieces or use a narrower clasp.

BRACELET SIZE	7.50"
SUBTRACT CLASP SPACE	- 1.50"
1/8" SPACE (.125)	
BETWEEN BEADS x 5	- .625"
	= 5.35"
DIVIDED BY 6 BEADS	= .892"

EACH BEAD MUST BE .892" WIDE

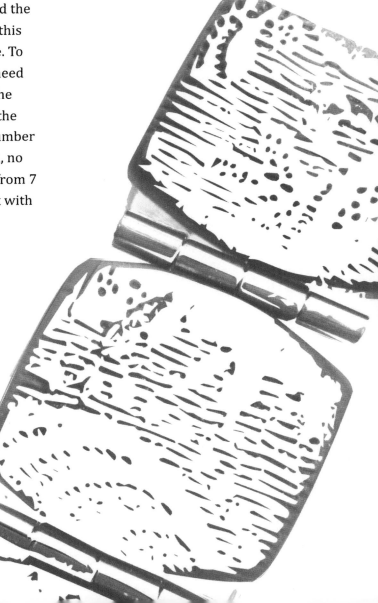

CUSTOM BRACELET FORMS

A BETTER BANGLE/CUFF

Many of us wear cuffs and bangle bracelets because we love their look. But when it comes to the fit, we are stuck with what manufacturers give us. Bulky bangle and cuff bracelets are fun to look at but not always comfortable to wear. The reason is, the amount of room necessary to enter the rigid bracelet requires that it be far bigger than your wrist. That often means it is so big, it gets in your way with each movement. I have had a love/hate relationship with bangles and cuffs for these very reasons. Then I had the idea to create something better.

THE BIKINI BANGLE

What I like to call the "Bikini Bangle", is a two piece bracelet. It pulls apart and clicks back together. You might be wondering what is gained with a two piece bangle and the answer is fit. Because my Bikini Bangle does not have to slip over your hand, it can be made smaller, a closer fit, eliminating the annoying aspects of a typical bulky bangle.

To further accommodate that idea, I came up with a simple way to create two nicely shaped bracelet forms that can be personalized for the size of your wrist.

One is a 1.50" wide slightly curved personal bangle bracelet form. You can use it to create the Top Mount Magnet Bangle on page 74, the Side Mount Magnet Bangle on page 76, the Hardware Loop Wrap bracelet on page 82 and any of the spring hinge bracelets in this book.

The second form is 2" and very curved. Both bracelet forms are made in the same basic way. The width of the clay and the curvature of the base used for shaping, give the wide bracelet lots more bend in the wall of the form, and ultimately your finished bracelet.

Your wrist size will determine the base needed to create your personal form. Glass votive holders, wine glasses, glass tree ornaments, burned out light bulbs and even perfectly shaped apples can be used if their size is right for you! Other fruits and vegetables might also work but I have not experimented with anything but an apple. Do not eat the baked apple or consume any food that has been in contact with clay!

CUSTOM BRACELET FORMS

CREATING YOUR FORM

Find a base for your form. It could be a votive holder, a glass ornament, a light bulb, an apple or any object that measures about one inch larger than your wrist. It should have an evenly curved shape.

1 - Sheet scrap clay on the pasta machine's #1 setting. Cut a strip the desired width and length and slightly longer than your base. Wrap the clay around the base.

2 - Match straight edges and cut off excess but do not blend the seam permanently because you will cut it open later.

3 - Cup the clay in your hands to press the top and bottom edges to the form. You only have to create this once because you will be able to use this form repeatedly to make several style bracelets. Make sure the shaping is smooth and even.

4 - When using a glass tree ornament, create a stand for curing it in the oven by jamming a craft stick into a clump of scrap clay. Insert the stick into the ornament to hold it upright while baking.

5 - Cure the clay.

6 - While the clay is still warm (not hot) slice open the joined seam with a craft knife or tissue blade and remove it from the glass. Hold the shape together and dip it in cold water until it becomes rigid and cool.

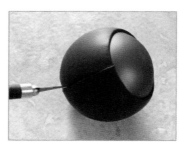

When using an apple as your base, allow it to cool. The fruit will give when touched but will not lose its shape or become soft. When cooled, use a craft knife to split the seam and remove the clay.

CREATING YOUR FORM

7 - If the size of the clay makes a good personal fit for you, you do not have to do anything but join the seam again with masking tape and cover the form in foil. Carefully smooth out every wrinkle of foil possible especially around the curved edges.

If the bangle is too big, determine how much needs to be trimmed from the sliced seam. Measure and mark the clay. Use a craft knife to slice and remove the section. Use masking tape to join the two new ends. Cover the adjusted form in foil.

You now have a very personalized fit for your two piece bangle or cuff bracelet designed with magnets, hinges or other elements. The possibilities are endless.

Keep in mind that you can also create thin cuffs with these instructions that don't require hinges or even two pieces! Roll out your clay on setting #2. Once cured, the clay will be flexible enough to slip on and off provided you leave about a one inch gap between the ends. If you want the front edges to overlap, add more clay on each end and be sure to place card stock between the pieces while the clay is curing to prevent them from bonding. This is how the wrap bracelet on page 82 was created.

DESIGNED WITH CUSTOM FORMS

pg. 46

pg. 48

pg. 74

pg. 76

pg. 80

pg. 82

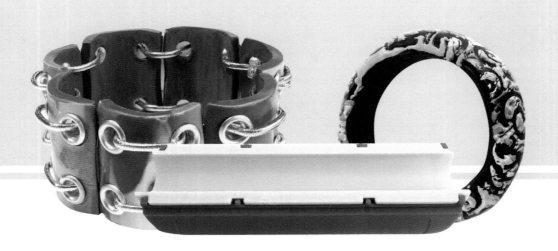

EASY BARREL AND HALF TUBE BEADS

Barrel Beads

Curved bracelet beads can be created in many ways. One of the easiest and most convenient I have found is using the Sculpey Bead Maker kit. The intent of the of the "U" shaped tool included in the kits, is to help you create uniform round beads. It does that exceptionally well. I have discovered the tool is also ideal for designing different size barrel beads.

1 - Mist the tool and fill it with scrap clay. Pack it down tightly.

2 - Use a tissue blade to slice off the excess so that the clay tube is level with the top of the tool and the ends.

3 - Remove the clay from the tool and cure it.

4 - Wrap the clay with foil or parchment paper. Cut your bead clay to the length you want and drape the pieces over the tube. Trim the clay edges and cure the beads.

Sculpey offers the Bead Maker tool in three sizes - 13mm, 16mm, and 18mm. The variety makes it convenient to create beads and bracelet forms in three widths and curvatures. The Stretchy Barrel Bead bracelet on page 66 used this technique.

Half Round Bangles

The Bead Maker kit is also ideal for shaping perfect bangle bracelets. Follow steps 1 - 3 for creating two tubes. Before curing, join them, then wrap them around a bracelet form. Drape a thin sheet of textured or colored clay over the tube if desired.

Wrap a strip of parchment paper around the clay and secure it with tape to hold the tube in place while curing. This technique was used for the Side Mount Magnet Bangle on page 76.

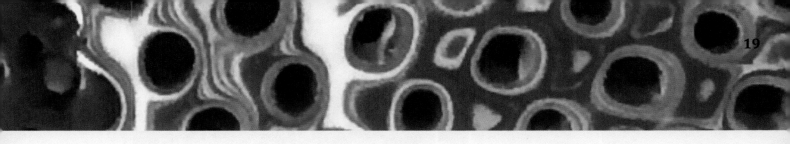

MOKUME´ GANE´ TOOLS

Many artists who use the Mokumé Gané technique in their work find their own favorite approach for setting up and slicing thin layers from a stack of clay. I have seen the stack attached to glass, wood blocks treated with a non-slip finish, and clever structured contraptions that insure each slice will be uniform in thickness.

Sculpey Design blocks are made to impress patterns into clay. They work well to create Mokumé Gané designs.

I recently discovered another purpose for them. A clay stack to be textured can be mounted on the flat side of a Sculpey design block. They measure a little more than 1.25" x 3.25". If you do not make beads wider than 1.25", the block is an ideal size for bracelet beads. It will allow you to create one complete slice to cover one bead.

Cut a thick, extra clay layer measuring 1" wider than the block. Wrap the ends around the edges.

Position your stack on top and add texture to the clay with various tools. The teeth of the block will grip the extra clay and hold the stack completely stable.

Clay artists typically use a tissue blade to slice thin sheets from the stack. A potato peeler is my choice for this job. I like the control it offers. Unless I am accidentally tilting it to one side, the peeler will cut a uniform slice.

The beauty of the block is that it works well in conjunction with the peeler. The block raises the clay off the surface allowing me to shave nearly to the bottom of the clay stack without the edges of the plastic peeler touching the work surface. The clay does not budge and identical slices are easy to achieve.

CLAY AND THE STENCIL CUTTING MACHINE

If you own a stencil cutting machine or plan to buy one, you will be excited to know that you can cut clay on some stencil machines. I have owned two machines from Silhouette America, my latest being the Cameo. That is my only reference for this topic.

I am currently cutting clay on my machine after reading an eye-opening tutorial on Sculpey.com. Sculpey's page also offers a video. Combined they offer you everything you need to know about cutting clay on the stencil machine. On the site, click the "Create" button then the "Home Decor" button to view the beautiful Souffle Bowl by Mags Bonham which was cut on the Cameo.

I have been using a stencil machine for several years. I initially bought mine because I do a lot of airbrush painting and was not happy with the stencils available commercially. The machine and its incredibly complete software allowed me the ability to design my own stencils, with any theme. I found that text, as well as images turned out precisely as I imagined them. The software was used to create this entire book from cover to cover!

Fast forward several years and today I have the same opportunity to apply my own designs to clay projects. I can cut anything I imagine into clay using the machine.

The implications of combining the stencil machine tool with clay are so enormous, it is difficult to imagine all the possibilities.

The Details

Is everything perfect when cutting clay on the machine? Not always. The good news is that unless you are cutting really tiny shapes, you can expect great results. Nevertheless at the outset, there are details that must be addressed.

• It is a very good idea to have a dedicated blade and mat for cutting clay. You do not want paper projects to be tinted by clay from a previous clay cut job.

• Always adhere freezer paper or wax paper to the mat and lay the clay on top of it.

• Move the metal coils on the cutting machine bar out to the sides so they do not come in contact with the clay.

• Be sure to position your cut image on the computer screen to match the position of your clay on the mat. The grid on the mat make this easy.

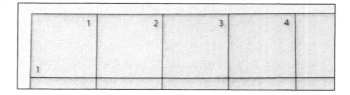

• Set the stencil cutter blade (using the ratchet) to "0" or the number "1" setting. Unscrew the white end of the blade. Put the unit back into the machine.

• On the "Cut" page of the software, go to "Material Type". Set up a new menu item called "Clay".

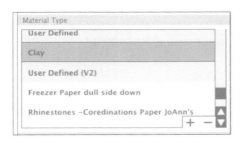

• In the "Edit" menu, set the speed at "8" and the thickness at "2".

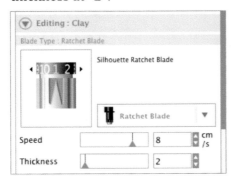

With this new menu item, you can easily click on "Clay" and not have to change the settings each time you are cutting clay with the machine.

• The clay should be a medium thickness to cut properly. On the Sculpey pasta machine, that would be a number five setting.

Overly soft clay can be a problem. If your clay seems soft or sticky, roll it out on the suggested setting. Position it on the cutting mat, then place it in the refrigerator for a while. After it is firmer, send it to be cut.

• Before removing the cut pieces it is a good idea to first place freezer paper, parchment or bakers paper on the clay. Flip it over and remove the backing by rolling it away instead of just pulling it off, which might stretch the clay.

• With finely detailed designs, hold positive pieces down with a clay sculpting tool while you remove the negative pieces so they do not tear adjoining clay or alter the shape.

What Can You Cut?

Almost any appropriately sized project can be cut on the stencil machine. Text that is linked and most images are not a problem. Really fine details might be an issue which has little to do with the machine's cutting ability and a lot to do with the user's patience for removing the negative pieces. Keep in mind that clay is a malleable medium. You can easily correct any mistakes by touching up or mending pieces with sculpting tools.

Very little in the way of design is beyond your reach. Consider that you can copy a simple Google image, bring it into your stencil cutting program, trace it, and cut it into clay. Oh the possibilities!

The Leather Snap Strap bracelet on page 84 was cut with the Cameo Stencil cutting machine.

BRACELET PROJECT CATEGORIES

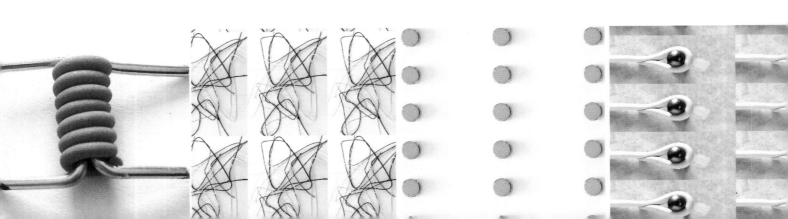

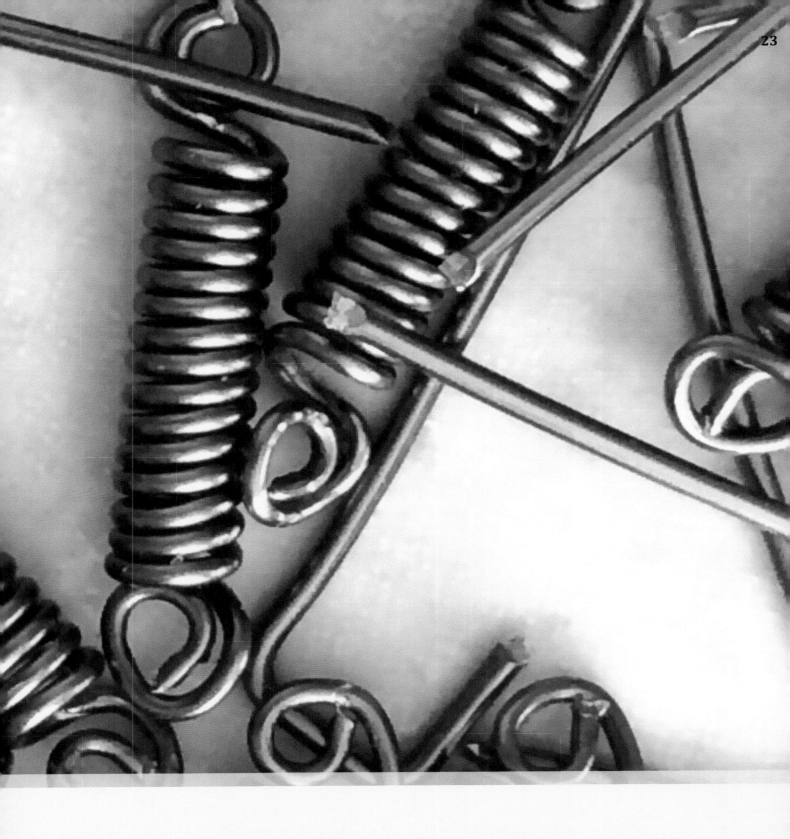

WIRE

Gold Wire Lifesavers

Wire • Mold • Skinner Blend • General Blend • Bracelet Measures 7.50"

1

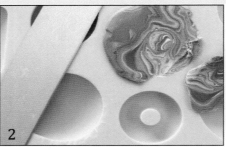

2

3

Prepare the Fuchsia and Yellow skinner blend and a Spanish Olive and White blend. Cut the clay blends into 3" squares. Stack all the squares and use a general blend technique to mix the colors.

Mist the medium cabochon mold. Press the clay into the mold. Slice away excess with a tissue blade positioned almost perpendicular to the mold. Save the colorful scraps for another project.

Pop the clay out of the mold. Create a total of seven beads. Cure the beads.

4

5

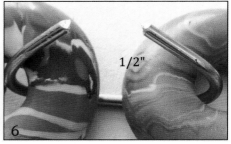

6

1/2"

Sand and buff the clay to a sheen. If you are using a rotary tool, secure the bead with a pipe cleaner you can hold onto to prevent it from sailing across the room.

Cut six pieces of wire to measure two inches. Cut another to measure one inch. Slip a two inch wire into a bead. Curl the end just slightly to the center of the wire. Slip the other wire end into the next bead.

Curve the wires to cross in the center. Do not press them flat. Allow 1/2" between beads for movement. Trim both wires in the center with a 1/8" space between them.

SUPPLIES

Premo
Fuchsia
Yellow
Spanish Olive
White
Cabochon Mold

Gold wire 16 – 18 gauge
Jewelry Glue
Crimp Beads

7mm Jump rings

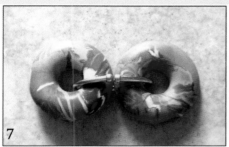

7

8

9

Slide crimp beads onto the wires. If they slide loosely on the wire, coat the wire ends with jewelry glue then position the crimp beads. Press the wire ends down so the crimp beads meet.

Curve the one inch wire over an object like a magic marker to form it into a "C" shape.

Attach three jump rings to the wire and connect it to the bar end of a toggle clasp. Slip crimp beads onto the ends of the wires and press them together.

10

To clasp the bracelet, slip the toggle bar through the last bead in the strand. The bar should be long enough so that it does not pass through the bead hole easily. The hole in the medium cabochon measures 5/16" and works well with a .75" bar.

What can you do with all those beautiful scraps?

Once you finish with your bracelet, you will have two different kinds of clay remaining - the large blended pieces from cutting the initial squares, and wildly patterned pieces which resulted in slicing off the tops of the cabochons. All the clay should be saved for future projects.

Your leftovers can be used in many interesting ways. Press them into a rubber stamp to create a Sutton Slice or stack them and press objects into them for a Mokume Gane project. You can also pass them through the conditioning machine on a very thin setting. The colors will stretch, giving you yet another variation on the blends you can achieve with this color mix.

Thin scraps of the clay were pressed onto a single sheet of clay to cover this business card case. After applying the clay to the top, the case was flipped over onto plastic wrap. The excess was removed using a tissue blade held at an angle which created a beveled edge on all sides. The clay was then cured on the case and later buffed to a high sheen.

Wired Under The Sea

Wire • Template • General Blend • Bracelet Measures 7.50"

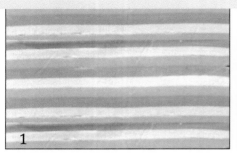

1

Roll clay on #1 setting. Cut a 4" square from each color and stack them - blue, white and green. Cut the stack in half and stack again in the same color order. Cut in half and stack one more time. Press together.

2

Roll the clay into a tube and do a general blend until you like the results. Sheet the clay on the #5 setting of the pasta machine.

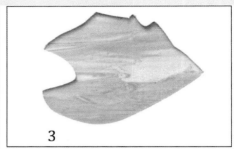

3

Use the template on page 86 and a craft knife to cut out six blended fish shapes.

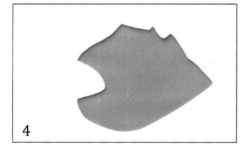

4

Roll out one ounce of the blue clay on the #2 setting. Set the fish template on the clay and cut out six shapes using a craft knife.

5

Place the shortened fish shape on the clay and with a sharp object draw a vertical line on the clay where the template ends.

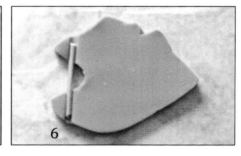

6

Cut a .50" piece of wire and press it onto the vertical line. Press only hard enough to create a depression in which the wire can rest.

SUPPLIES

Premo
Turquoise
Wasabi
White
Liquid Polymer
Etch 'N Pearl tool
Comb tool

16 gauge wire
8/0 Aqua Delica Beads
5 & 10 mm jump rings

Small brush
Magnetic Clasp
Blue and Green Mica Powder

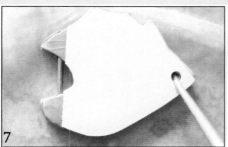

7

Set the blended clay on the turquoise clay. Use the template as a guide for the eye placement. Use the Etch N' Pearl tool to create a hole large enough to easily accommodate the jump ring.

8

With a sharp object, draw a line from the top front of the fish to the back. Create definition in the fins with a comb tool. Place the round end of the Etch N' Pearl tool at an angle on the clay and gently press down to create fish scales.

9

With a dry brush, apply blue mica powder followed by a touch of green.

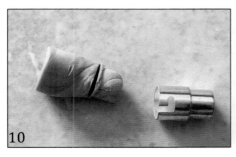

10

Roll two pieces of the blended clay in your hands. Stuff them into each clasp opening. Mark the clay where the clasp ends. This is how deep the plug should be. Pull the clay out. Trim it on the mark.

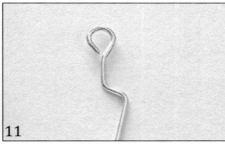

11

Create a couple of bends in two eyepin wires with pliers. Trim them so the final length of each wire is not longer than the plug.

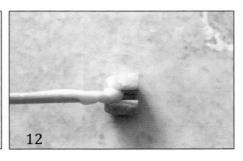

12

Slice open the plugs slightly. Apply liquid polymer to the inside walls.

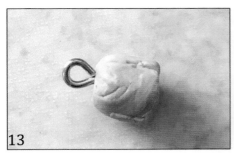

13

Lay the wire inside the opening. Press together. Apply liquid polymer inside the clasp. Push the plug into the clasp. Cure the clay.

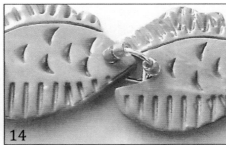

14

To assemble the bracelet, slip a 10mm jump ring through the fish eye. Add three beads.

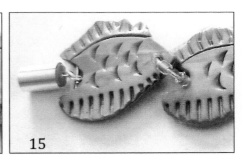

15

Insert the jump ring through the straight wire of another fish and close the ring. Attach the clasp pieces with 5mm jump rings.

Coiled Wire Cane

Wire • Template • Cane • Skinner Blend • Bracelet Measures 7.75"

Cut two pieces of clay measuring four inches square from burnt umber and one square the same size from fuchsia and orange. Create Skinner Blends with the combined colors as shown. Stack like colors on top of each other.

Roll the blended fuchsia and umber pieces on the #5 setting to produce a long thin sheet. Repeat with the orange and umber.

Fold each sheet accordion style about 1" wide.

Shape the piece by pushing in from the sides. Press the top flat. Turn it and press and keep turning until you have a compact rectangle that measures about 2" x .75", enough to cover the size of a bead.

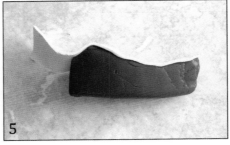

Mix white with ecru to lighten it and sheet it on the #5 setting. Use blades to cut curved vertical shapes from each color rectangle. Remove the cut shapes from the rectangles and place the ecru strip against the cut wall.

Replace the matching cut pieces. Press together and trim the Ecru piece to conform to the rectangle.

SUPPLIES

Premo
Burnt umber
Ecru
White
Fuchsia
Orange
Liquid polymer

Potato peeler
Clasp
20 gauge antique brass wire
7mm jump rings

3/32" drill bit
Wood block
Sharpie marker

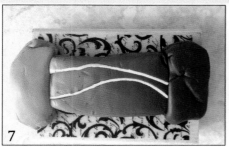

Place a rectangle on a wood block. Border the ends with rolls of clay roughly shaped to match the stack's height and color. Press them to the stack ends. The "bumpers" are a buffer for starting and finishing the clay slicing.

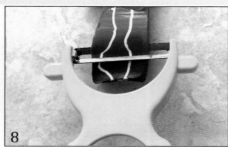

Use a potato peeler to shave thin slices from the rectangles. You will need five fuchsia and five orange slices. Cut a few more than you need for insurance.

Roll out burnt umber clay on # 2 setting. The piece should be large enough to cut the ten beads necessary for the bracelet. Place the orange and fuchsia color slices on the solid color clay.

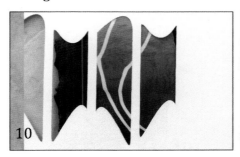

Position the templates on the ten bead blends. Use a craft knife to cut out the shapes. You will find the templates on page 86.

With a Sharpie, mark a piece of wire at .25", then at 1.25", then at 1.50". Cut the wire on the last line. Create 18 wires with the same markings. Make one 90 degree bend in each wire at the .25" mark.

Create the nine coils by wrapping wire around the base of a 3/32" drill bit until the coil is .50" long. Leave .50" tails on each end.

With round nose pliers, curl the ends of the coil.

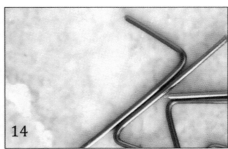

Slip two 1.25" wires into each coil, then bend 90 degree angles at the 1.25" mark in each to form a "U" shape wire.

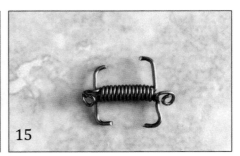

Pinch the top and bottom "U" shape wires with pliers to make them level. One edge should not be sticking up higher than another.

16

17

18

Create backing pieces by rolling a strip of burnt umber clay on the #4 setting. Cut it to measure .75" wide. Cut out ten .50" rectangles from the strip. Place a rectangle under a hinge wire, then the another under the parallel wire.

Continue adding backing pieces in a line. Use a craft stick to apply liquid polymer generously over the "U" shape wires.

Place the skinner blend beads over the backing and wires. Press together.

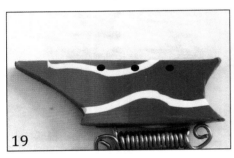

19

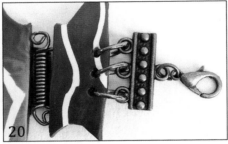

20

Align a three strand clasp with the two end beads. Pierce three holes into the clay to match the clasp holes. Cure the beads.

Sand and buff the beads. Open jump rings and insert them into the holes. Connect the claps pieces and close the jump rings.

NOTE
Canes can be sliced with either a tissue blade or a potato peeler. Go to page 19 to read how you can raise the clay up off the work surface to make slicing easier whichever tool you use.

If you do not have a design block to support your stack, the back of a large rubber stamp may provide the height you need.

Each clay slice will have a slightly different look. Flip the slices over to determine if you like the backsides better than the fronts.

CHAIN & JUMP RINGS

Three Strand Twist

Chain • Extruded • Bracelet Measures 7.50"

1

Feed turquoise clay into the extruder fitted with a seven hole disc. Press out enough tubing to measure at least 7" long. Do the same with the green clay, then the ultramarine blue.

2

Hold the ends of three tubes stationary while you gently roll the remainder of the tubes away from you on the work surface with your other hand. This will twist the tubes around each other evenly.

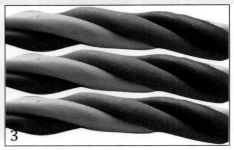

3

Cut the twist into three pieces measuring 2" long.

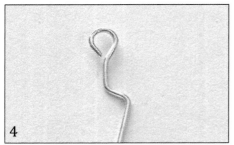

4

Use needle nose pliers to create two opposing bends in an eye pin wire.

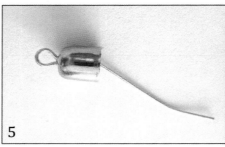

5

Insert the eye pin into an end cap. Use wire cutters to cut away wire extending beyond the edge of the cap. With a toothpick, apply Liquid Polymer to the inside of the cap and the wire.

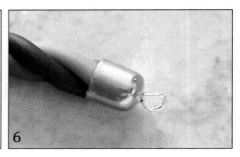

6

Slightly squeeze the end of a twisted clay piece. Insert it into the cap. Once it is planted inside, push down on the eye pin wire to imbed it into the clay. Repeat on the other end of the twist. Create three of these sections.

Supplies

Premo
Turquoise
Green
Ultramarine blue
Liquid polymer

End cap with 5mm or more opening
Lobster clasp
Eye pin wires
Chain

Extruder

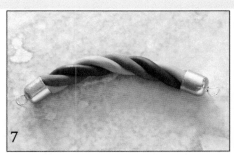

7

Curve the sections slightly. Less curve is needed for a large wrist. The curve will cause the bracelet to follow the bend of your wrist. Cure the clay.

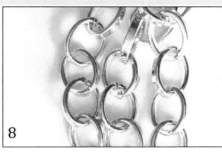

8

Cut 6 pieces of chain to measure 2.50" long.

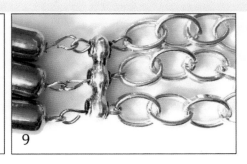

9

Connect an eye pin to each chain. Pass the eye pin wire through a three hole spacer and create a loop in the wire. Before closing the loop, attach it to the loop in the end cap.

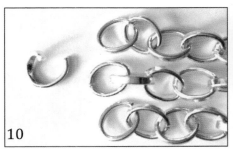

10

Open a chain link and connect it to the last three chain lengths on each side of the bracelet to join them.

11

Connect a lobster clasp to the link on one side. The clasp will attach to the single link on the other side of the bracelet.

NOTE

Clay should be well conditioned before inserting it into an extruder. Look for air bubbles and get rid of them by stretching the clay before beginning. Bubbles in the clay may remain in the extruded material or cause breaks in the surface.

Clean the interior and the disc when changing clay to prevent contamination of colors.

Attaching a vise to a counter top to hold your extruder makes easy work of expelling clay with any style discs.

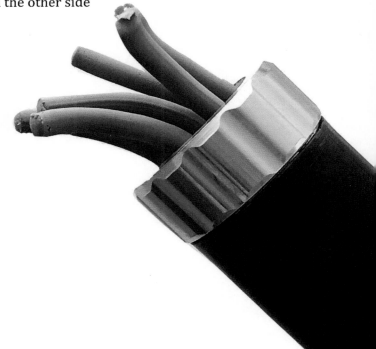

Chained Chiclet

Chain • Blended • Bracelet Measures 6.50"

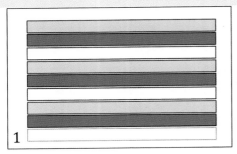

1

Roll each clay color on the #1 setting. Use a 4" cutter to create equal size squares. Stack them alternating blue, green and white. Cut the square in half and stack it. Cut again and stack.

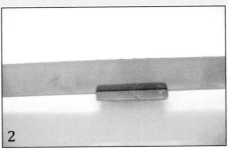

2

Cut through the stack from top to bottom slicing .50" wide pieces. Roll each slice into a tube with your hands. Use the general blending technique to mix the colors. Roll out the blended color pieces on #1 setting.

3

Cover the clay with plastic wrap. Using a .75" cutter push down on the clay. Create seven beads. Cut extras so you will have a choice of color patterns.

4

Cut a .75" paper template with dots equally spaced in the four corners. Using the template, pierce holes in the beads with an Etch 'N Pearl tool. Make the holes slightly larger than the diameter of the jump rings.

5

Using the Etch 'N Pearl tool, pierce two holes in two end beads to attach the clasp. Align the clasp with the bead to mark the hole placement. Cure the beads.

6

Place the beads on plastic or aluminum foil to apply glaze. Before the application, place toothpicks or jewelry wire in the bead holes to keep them from collecting glaze and sealing up.

SUPPLIES

Premo
Blue Pearl
Spanish Olive
White
Etch 'N Pearl tool
Liquid polymer

Square clay cutters 4" & .75"
Two strand magnetic clasp
8" length fancy chain
7mm & 10mm jump rings

Plastic wrap
Glaze

7

8

9

Remove the toothpicks. Open two 10mm jump rings and insert them into one side of a bead.

Cut a three link piece of fancy chain.
Insert the jump rings through the top and bottom chain links, then into the holes on another bead. Close the rings.

Connect the remainder of the beads using the jump rings and chain.

10

The two end beads have two holes for attaching the clasp pieces. Insert the 7mm jump rings to connect the clasps to the beads. Cut two link pieces of chain (not three like the rest of the bracelet) and attach them to the jump rings before closing them.

NOTE
Three links of chain should measure approximately .75" long. If your chain links are a different size make adjustments to the chain pieces accordingly.

All the beads in the bracelet are connected to each other with 10mm jump rings. The clasps are attached with 7mm rings.

If the diameter of the holes in the beads are not large enough, the bracelet will be rigid and unable to flex freely.

Beads can be cut with a tissue blade instead of a square cutter, but the edges won't be beveled. Gently press a credit card against the edges at a slight angle to round the sharp edges.

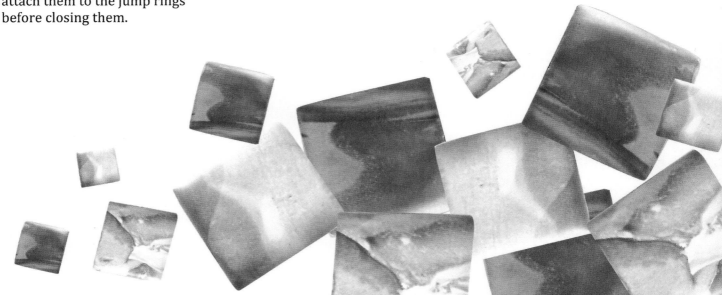

ABOUT HARDWARE HINGES

Pretty hardware hinges for bracelets are not as readily available as you might expect. Although an internet search will reveal many hinges, you will find most are either too industrial looking or much too big for a bracelet. Not-so-pretty versions can be hidden on the back of clay or embedded so they don't distract from beautiful clay designs.

There are many books available and websites offering instructions to walk you through the steps of making your own metal hinges. But if you are looking for a hinge without having to do the metal work, you can find a few unusual hinges where I have found most of mine - at eBay, Etsy, or Hobby Lobby. Look in my Tools and Supplies section for details.

I do not feel this book would be complete without offering you alternative hinges, ones you can create yourself. You have already seen some in the "Wire" section of this book. You will also see other examples in "Clay Connections" on page 51. I especially want to bring to your attention the custom hinge used for the "Birds On A Wire" bracelet on page 52. It is unique because it is a hinge in every sense of the word, except it is made with clay instead of metal. It mimics the structure of the traditional metal hinges you will see in the following section, but a piece of wire acts as the hinge pin. With a little imagination, this hinge concept can be applied to many bracelet designs when you cannot find ready made metal ones.

I have used glass tube beads as well as finishing nails in place of wire as hinge pins. Take a trip to your local hardware store. It might reveal even more options for custom hinges!

HARDWARE HINGES

Copper Front Mount Hinge

Hardware Hinge • Blended • Bracelet Measures 7 3/8"

Cut equal size clay pieces from ecru and copper rolled on the #1 setting. Stack, cut in half and repeat.

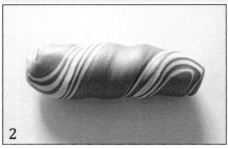

Roll the clay on the work surface with your hands and blend.

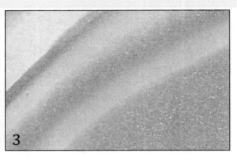

When you are happy with the blend, cut six rectangles to measure 2" x 1 1/8". Plan your cuts to take advantage of most colorful marbled areas.

Roll solid ecru clay on the #2 setting. Trace the hinge shape onto the clay with a craft knife. Cut 10 pieces.

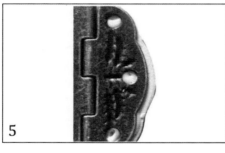

Apply Liquid Polymer to the back side of the hinges. Press them to the ecru pieces allowing the clay to protrude slightly beyond the scalloped hinge edge.

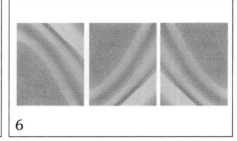

Place all the blended squares on your work surface with the top edges aligned. Cut the bottoms evenly with a blade to measure 1.25" long. Leave 1/8" space between the beads for the hinge backs.

SUPPLIES

Premo
Copper
Ecru
Etch 'N Pearl tool
Liquid polymer

Antique gold wire 16 gauge
8mm Antique gold jump rings
Antique gold end caps 1/25" long
5 Antique hinges 1.25" long

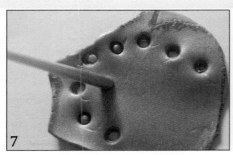

7

Cut six solid copper dots for each hinge using the small Etch 'N Pearl tool.

8

Arrange the hinges on the clay rectangles. Use a toothpick dipped in Liquid Polymer to pierce the holes in the hinges. Lightly press the copper dots over the holes so they come in contact with the Liquid Polymer.

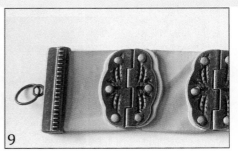

9

As you arrange your hinges, keep in mind that the rectangles on both ends of the bracelet have a hinge on only one edge.

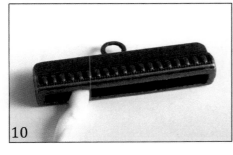

10

Insert Liquid Polymer into the openings of the end caps followed by the clay rectangle edges. Cure the bracelet.

11

Fold the wire in half and wrap it around a small object like a pen to create a .50" "S" shape.

12

Close one end of the "S" around a jump ring attached to the end cap. Leave an opening in the other end of the "S" to act as a hook. Attach a copper jump ring to the second end cap. Sand the rough straight edges of the rectangles. Sand and buff the bracelet beads.

NOTE
Review the information in "Things To Remember" on page 10 concerning top mounted hinges.

You can find decorative hinges appropriately sized for bracelets on Etsy and eBay.

Gold Embedded Hardware Hinge

Hardware Hinge • Blended • Texture Sheet • Gold Foil • Bracelet Measures 6.50"

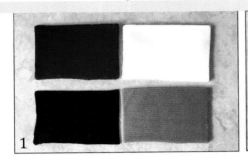

Roll out rose gold, crimson, and white clay on #1 setting. Roll black on #5 setting. Cut all clay colors into four inch squares.

Apply gold foil to the crimson clay following package instructions.

Stack the squares with the black on top, then crimson, white, and rose gold. Cut the stack in half and put one on top of the other using the same color order. Cut and stack one more time.

Blend the stack and roll the clay on the #3 setting.

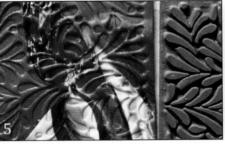

Press a rubber stamp or texture sheet all over the blended clay to transfer the design.

Cut the beads to measure .75" x 1" with a clay cutter or tissue blade. Cut seven each from the blended clay and from crimson clay rolled on the #2 setting.

SUPPLIES

Premo
Rose gold
Crimson
White
Black
Liquid Polymer

Gold foil
Clasp
Rubber stamp or texture sheet

.75" x 1" clay cutter
1" hinges

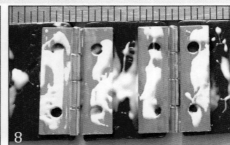

Place parchment paper on the work surface. Tape down a ruler above it. On the paper, line up the tops of the crimson beads to the bottom of the ruler. Position the hinges between the beads with hinge pins facing down.

Once you are happy with the alignment of the pieces, remove the hinges. Don't move the clay. Apply liquid polymer to the edges of the clay. Replace the hinges, pin side up. Apply liquid polymer to the surface of the hinges.

Create clasp loops by cutting two pieces from the blended and textured clay to measure 1" x 5/8".

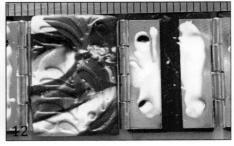

Slip the loop pieces into the clasp sides. Fold to bring the clay ends together. Press the ends to reduce the bulk at the edges.

Position the clasp loops on the two end beads of the bracelet.

Place the blended and textured clay rectangles over the crimson clay with tops and bottoms matching.

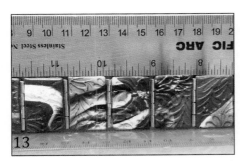

Press a ruler flush against the bottoms of the beads to be sure they all line up evenly. Cure the clay. Buff the finished beads.

NOTE
The black clay is rolled thinner than the other colors so it doesn't overpower the blend giving it a dark look.

The amount of gold visible in the final bracelet will be determined by the blend, how deep the texture is and how much you buff the beads.

Front Mount Barrel Bead Hinge

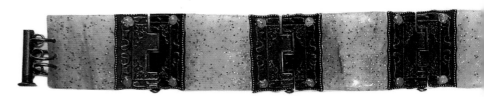

Hardware Hinge • Translucent Clay blended with Alcohol Ink • Bracelet Measures 7.50"

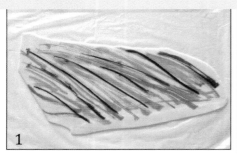

1 Roll clay on #2 setting. Gently drag alcohol pens across the clay. Alcohol inks can also be used. The final color of the beads will be determined by the most dominant color streaks on the clay.

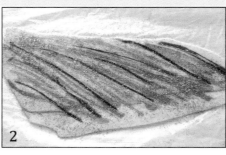

2 Sprinkle gold glitter on the center of the clay.

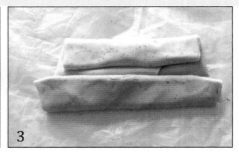

3 Wrap it into a package jelly roll style to enclose the glitter.

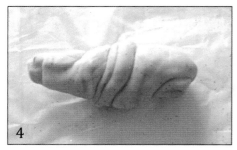

4 Blend the package. The more you roll and twist the clay, the more the colors will blend, creating less detail. Monitor the blending carefully to avoid this.

5 Use a cutter or tissue blade to create five 1" x 1.50" beads. Cut the two end beads to measure 1" x 1.25".

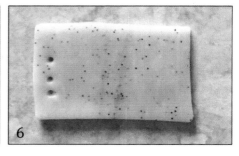

6 Make three small holes with the Etch 'N Pearl tool for the jump rings to attach to the two shorter beads.

SUPPLIES

Premo
Translucent
Etch 'N Pearl Tool
Liquid polymer

Spectrum Noir colors:
OR2, JG6, TN5, CR8
1" hinges
Gold or green glitter

Clasp
7mm jump rings

7

Place the bead pieces on a bracelet form to give them a barrel shape. See the information on page 15 for creating your own bracelet forms. Cure the beads then sand and buff to a high gloss.

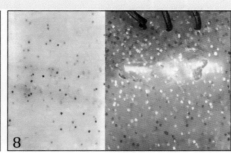

8

Working with translucent clay and alcohol inks is interesting. While you can plan your colors, you are often surprised by the result. This photo shows the dramatic change that raw clay (left) and cured clay (right) undergo.

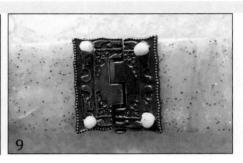

9

Apply liquid polymer to the back of the hinges and place them between the beads. Using the smallest etch n Pearl tool, shape dots to cover the holes in the hinges. Be sure the dots come in contact with liquid polymer.

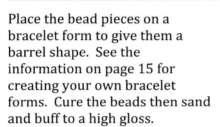

10

Cure the bracelet again on parchment paper. Apply glaze to the dots with a small brush.

11

Attach jump rings to the holes on the end beads and add the clasp.

Amazing Translucent Clay

Would you be believe it if I told you the stone look pendant on the left used the same translucent clay and the same ink colors as the bracelet project on these two pages? While identical colors were used, heavier application of certain colors made a wildly different look in the completed jewelry piece. Color application and the amount of clay manipulation during the blending process can create surprising results. I have never begun a project using the translucent /alcohol ink technique and come away with exactly what I had expected!

If you noticed the super gloss on the pendant, it was achieved exclusively by sanding and buffing. Translucent clay has the ability to look like glass or stone when properly finished.

SPRING HINGES

Spring Hinge Front Hook

Spring Hinge • Extruded • 1.50" Bracelet Form

1

The clay for this bracelet came from the shavings from the Side Mount Bangle bracelet on page 75. Roll the shavings in your hand to form a tube. Feed it into the extruder.

2

Attach a seven hole disc to the extruder cap. Extrude the clay.

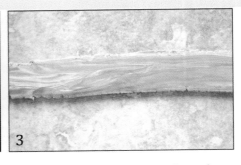

3

Create a base for the bracelet tubes by rolling scraps of clay on #1 setting. Cut the piece to measure .50" x 6" or larger according to your wrist size.

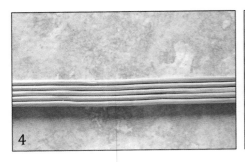

4

Arrange five tubes on the base. Cut them along the length into two equal pieces.

5

Brush liquid polymer on both sides of the hinge. Use a craft knife to separate .50" of the tubes from the base on both pieces. Insert the hinge pieces with the spring on the same side as the tubes. Press down to adhere the tubes, hinge and base.

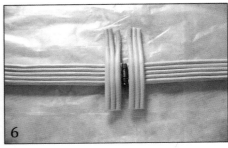

6

Gather three tubes together and wrap them on both sides of the hinge with the edges meeting on the base. Blend the tube seams together on the back side.

SUPPLIES

Premo
Blue
Wasabi
White
Liquid polymer

.50" spring hinge
Copper teardrop 1.50"
Copper wire 16 gauge

7mm jump rings
Extruder

7

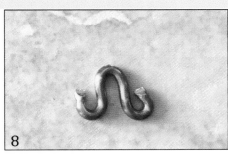

8

9

Press together three tubes and fold in half as one piece for the hook. Curl the folded end over. Attach it to a bracelet end. Wrap the connection with four tubes. Trim them so they meet on the back side of the bracelet.

Cut a piece of wire to hold the copper centerpiece. Fold it in half and curl the ends.

Apply liquid polymer to the curled wire ends. Press them into the clay so the loop just barely protrudes past the front edge. Wrap four tubes around the edge as you did for the other end in step 7. Wrap the bracelet on a form and cure.

10

11

12

Cut two pieces of copper wire to fit around the bracelet band behind the four wraps. With your fingers, bend the wire around the front of the clay.

Cut off excess and flatten the edges to the back. Copper wire scratches and dents easily, so use plastic nose pliers or regular pliers with padding covering the wire.

Sand the wire ends. On the wrong side of the bracelet, apply and flatten a dab of clay on the copper ends to protect you from any small sharp edges. Cure again. Sand the clay edges where necessary, then glaze.

Spring Hinge Open Front

Spring Hinge • Texture sheet • 1.50" Bracelet Form

1

Roll the clay on #1 setting. Create a piece twice as long as the size required for your wrist, and 1.50" wide.

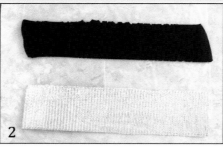

2

Mist the corrugated card stock. Place it on the clay and roll across it to transfer the ridge texture. Cut the clay length in half.

3

Apply silver mica powder to the raised areas of the clay with your finger or a brush. If powder falls into the recessed areas, run a fine brush dipped in alcohol across them to remove the powder.

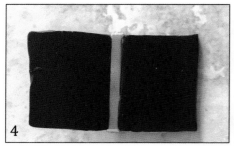

4

Cut two clay rectangles large enough to cover the spring hinge plates, about 1.25" by 1".

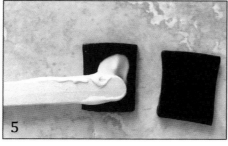

5

Apply liquid polymer to the squares.

6

Adhere the squares to the hinge plates on the sides opposite the spring.

SUPPLIES

Premo
Black
Liquid polymer

1" spring hinge
Clasp
Corrugated card stock
Silver mica powder
Small silver rivets

7

Press the corrugated clay pieces onto the opposite sides of the hinge plates. Position them close to the spring.

8

Place the clay on a bracelet form to shape it while curing.

9

Apply liquid polymer to two square silver rivets and press them into the front center edges.

10

Wrap a strip of parchment paper loosely around the clay to keep it shaped to the form. Wrapping too tightly will flatten the clay texture. Cure the clay. Sand rough edges and apply glaze.

Simple Spring Hinge

Spring Hinge Frame • Sutton Slice • 6.50"

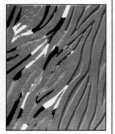

Mix red clay with periwinkle to create a deep navy color. Make a sutton slice by pressing bits of navy, gold glitter, and white into the rubber stamp. Shave the excess clay from the surface with a blade.

Roll out a four inch wide sheet of navy clay on setting #1. Press the sheet onto the rubber stamp. Carefully peel back the rubber stamp leaving the embedded shapes on the sheet.

With your hands, create two thick tubes of white clay. Press them into the frame until the frame is filled. Trim the excess clay away from the frame with a tissue blade. The inside clay should be flush with the frame.

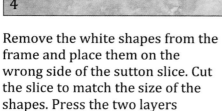

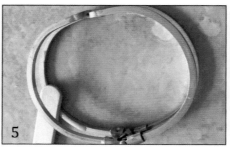

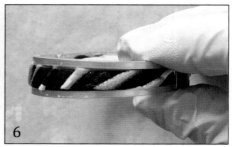

Remove the white shapes from the frame and place them on the wrong side of the sutton slice. Cut the slice to match the size of the shapes. Press the two layers together.

Use a craft stick to apply liquid polymer to the three inner edges of the metal frame on each bracelet panel.

Insert the two clay pieces into the frame from the inside until it is level with the front of the frame. Dip Q-tips in alcohol to remove liquid polymer that might have seeped onto the front of the metal. Trim the inside flush again if necessary. Cure the clay, then apply glaze.

Bracelet Frame Before

SUPPLIES

Premo
Periwinkle
White
Yellow Gold Glitter
Pomegranate
Liquid polymer

6.50" brass bracelet frame
Rubber stamp

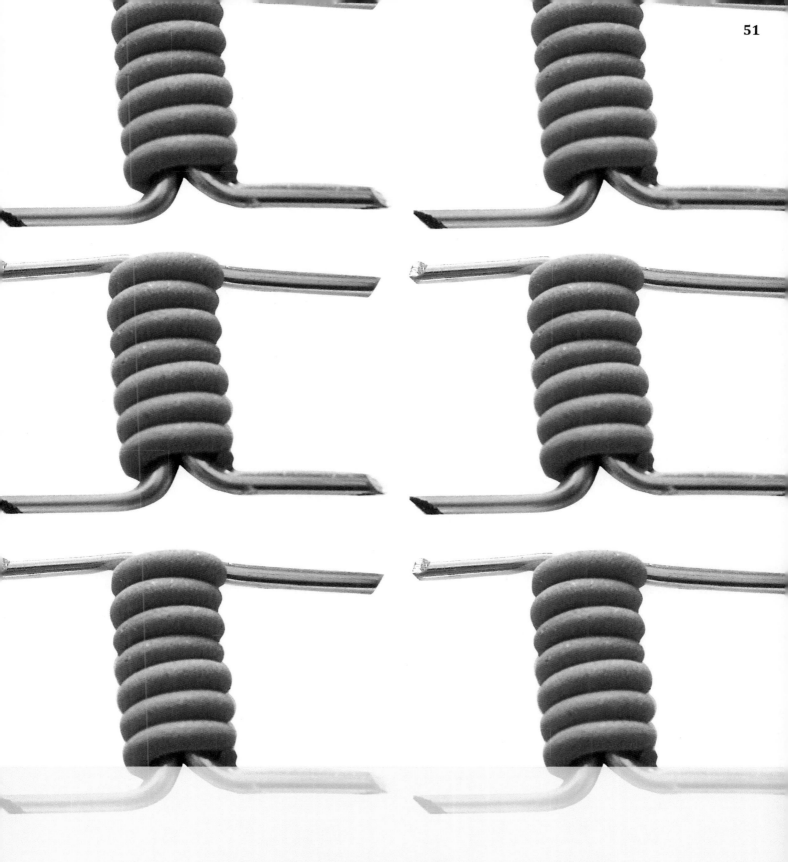

CLAY CONNECTIONS

Custom Birds On A Wire

Clay Hinge • Stencils & Templates • Bracelet Measures 7.50"

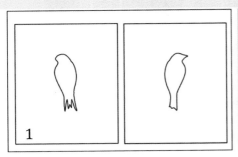

The stencil images for this project can be found on page 86. Use a craft knife or stencil cutting machine to cut the birds and bead templates from stencil blanks.

Roll black clay on #1 setting. Place a bird stencil on the clay. Use an acrylic roller to raise the clay to the surface.

Rub mica powder on the raised clay.

Carefully remove the stencil so powder doesn't fall onto the black surface. Wipe off the stencil so your next color is not contaminated by this one.

Position the left end bead template on the clay with the bird centered in the wide space. Cut the template shape with a tissue blade.

Remove the template. Place the clasp on the edge of the clay and mark holes for jump rings with an Etch 'N Pearl tool.

SUPPLIES

Premo
Black
Etch 'N Pearl Tool
Liquid polymer

Stencil blank
Clasp
18 gauge black wire
8mm black jump rings
Toothpicks

Mica powder color variety
Metallic silver marker

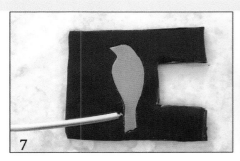

Press a curved piece of wire onto the bead to create the bird's perch.

Create the four interior beads and the right end bead. Choose a different color for each bird image.

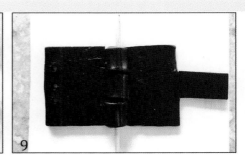

Place the beads image side down on parchment paper. Curl all of the bead extensions over toothpicks to shape them. Remove the picks. Fit the curled extensions together and reinsert the toothpick through all three "hinges".

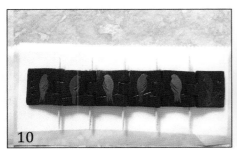

When all six beads are connected, place parchment paper on the back side of the bracelet and flip it right side up. Cure the beads on parchment paper.

Remove the toothpicks from the cured clay. If any of the clay parts were touching during curing, separate them using a craft knife. Lightly sand any rough spots if necessary.

Cut five 1" black wires. Slip them into the hinges. Use a large Etch 'N Pearl tool to create 10 rounded dots from the clay. Apply a little liquid polymer to each of the dots and press them to the ends of the hinges to trap the wires inside.

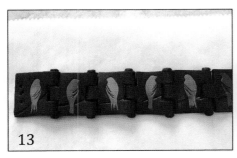

Return the bracelet to the oven again to cure.

Use a metallic silver marker to draw the wire lines on each bead.

Attach the clasp to the bracelet with black jump rings.

Extruded Spiral

Extruded Clay Spirals • Wire • Skinner Blend •Bracelet Measures 7.50"

1. Roll out both clay colors on the #1 setting. Create a 4" x 3" skinner blend with the orange and the green clay. Roll on the #2 setting.

2. Impress a texture tool onto the clay. Set aside.

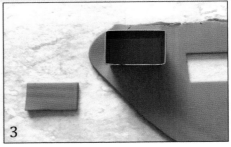

3. Roll out a sheet of solid orange approximately 4" x 3" on the #2 setting. Cut seven pieces with a .75" square cutter. Align the solid orange slices on the work surface.

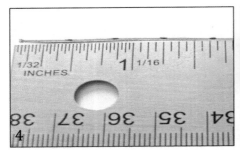

4. Mark a 10.50" wire with a Sharpie at 3/8" intervals. Remove the marks later with alcohol. Cut 14 pieces to measure .75". With pliers, create a 90-degree bend at only one of the marks on each wire to form an "L" shape.

5. Place a clump of orange clay in an extruder with a 12 hole disc. Extrude the clay.

6. Wrap clay tubes around a knitting needle, which is approximately the thickness of two 18 gauge wires. Cure the clay.

SUPPLIES

Premo
Celosia Orange
Margarita
Liquid Polymer

Texture tool
.75" square cutter
White Pearl mica powder
Extruder
Clasp

5mm jump rings
Sharpie Marker
Knitting Needle
18 gauge wire

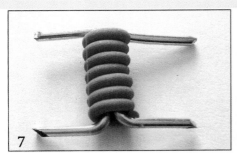

7

Slide the spiral wrap off the knitting needle and cut it with a craft knife into six pieces of about six wraps each. Insert the wires into the spirals. Bend the wires at the second mark to turn the "L" into a "U"shape.

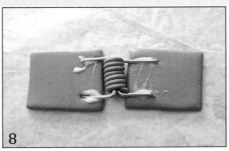

8

Apply liquid polymer to the squares. Press a set of wires onto each. Add wires until all the squares are linked with equal spacing. Bend the remaining two wires into a "U"; place them on the two end squares.

9

Cover the blended clay with plastic and use the cutter to produce seven squares. Press the blended squares over the glued hinges matching the orange clay edges. Press and smooth the seams of the squares together.

10

Brush the top ridges of the textured clay with White Pearl Mica powder. Cure the clay.

11

Attach three 5mm jump rings to the end wires and attach them to the clasp. Smooth the edges of the solid orange squares with sandpaper. Glaze the beads.

Tab Hinge

Clay Link • Mokumé Gané • Template • Bracelet Measures 7.75"

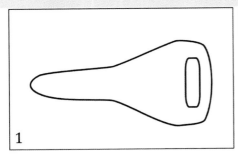

1 Print, and cut out the template from a stencil blank. You will find the template on page 87.

2 Cut four 4" squares of each color rolled on the #1 setting. Stack plum, green and blue. Cut in half, stack, and cut in half again. Stack with the same color order.

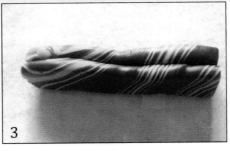

3 Roll the stack into a thick log. Twist and fold the log in half. Shape it into a log again.

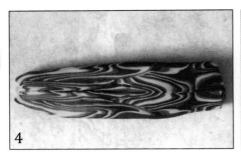

4 Cut the log in half along the length. Stick the two halves together matching the designs on each. Roll the blue clay into a tube shape to fill the crevice between the two logs on the underside.

5 Elevate the clay on a block of wood. Add clay "bumpers" on the two short ends that are the same height as the main clay. This will make shaving the clay easier. Use a potato peeler to shave thin slices off the top of the clay.

6 Roll out enough blue clay on the #2 setting to fit the template eight times. Place the shaved slices on the blue clay. Use the template to cut out eight pieces of the combined clay.

SUPPLIES

Premo
Robin's egg blue
Green
Plum
Liquid Polymer

Potato peeler
Clasp
10mm jump rings

Wood Block
Sharpie Marker

7

Bend the extension over a toothpick to curve it.

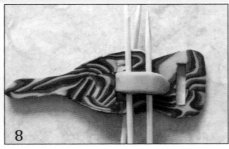

8

Slip the extension into the hole in another bead. Bend it toward the hole in its own bead so that the solid blue side is showing. Separate touching clay parts with toothpicks to keep them from bonding during curing.

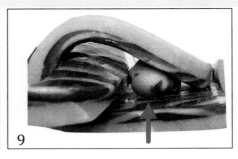

9

Roll small balls of scraps from the bracelet and place them under the tip of the extension to elevate it. The ball should not be visible. Press the clay and ball to the bead.

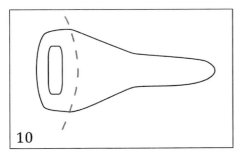

10

Create a special piece for the end of the bracelet using the template. Cut it the same as the other pieces then flip it over and cut the extension off. Shape it into an elongated "O".

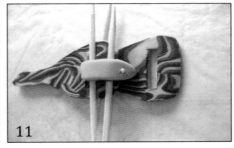

11

Shorten a silver ball head wire to a 1/2" stub. Holding it with pliers, dip it into liquid polymer. Pierce it into the end of the extension. Cure the bracelet.

12

Sand rough edges. Apply glaze. Attach three jump rings to the end pieces. Attach clasps to the rings.

Clay Link Watch

Clay • Texture Sheet • Adjustable

1 Roll white clay on the #1 setting. Cover the clay with baker's paper and use a 1 1/2" cutter to create two circles.

2 With a 1" cutter create a third circle and cut it in half.

3 Center a 1/2 " rectangular cutter on the straight edges and press through the clay.

4 Press a credit card on the straight edges to thin them.

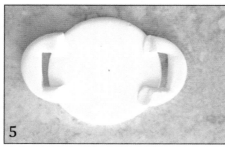

5 Align the two pieces on each side of one circle. Cover with the second circle.

6 Assemble the watch face and hands with the brad provided. Apply liquid polymer to the backside and center it on the circle.

SUPPLIES

Premo
White
Etch 'N Pearl tool
Liquid polymer

Tim Holtz watch face & parts
Rhinestones
Corrugated paper
Buckle

Various clay cutters
Gold mica powder
Credit card

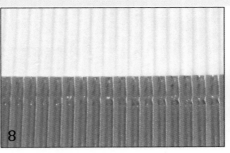

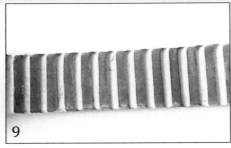

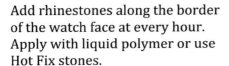

7

Add rhinestones along the border of the watch face at every hour. Apply with liquid polymer or use Hot Fix stones.

8

Roll an 8" long by 1" wide strip of white clay on the #5 setting. Mist corrugated foil then press it onto the strip.

9

Cut the clay strap to measure just under 1/2" wide. With your finger, apply mica powder to the raised areas of the strip. If some powder falls between the ridges blow it off or use a fine paint brush with alcohol to remove it.

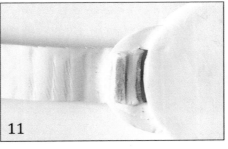

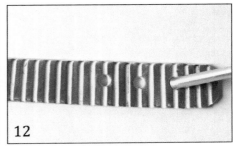

10

Thread the strap into the space in the watch extension. Apply liquid polymer to the top end of the strap. Press it to the back side of the extension.

11

After the strap is secure to the underside of the watch, trim it to 4" long.

12

Use the Etch 'N Pearl tool to make three holes in the strap.

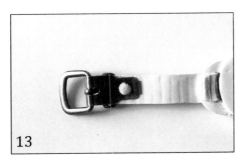

13

Use liquid polymer to attach the opposite strap as you did in step 10. Adjust the strap length to fit your wrist. Apply liquid polymer to the buckle. Adhere it to the end of the strap. With a medium Etch 'N Pearl tool, create a white dot. On the backside of the strap, press the dot into the hole in the hardware. Cure the clay right side up, then glaze it.

Strap Slider

Clay • Fabric Texture • Bracelet Measures 7.75"

1 — Roll clay on the #1 setting. Place the textured fabric on the clay and run it through the conditioning machine on the #2 setting.

2 — Place plastic wrap over the clay and cut 10 pieces with a 1" x 1.50" clay cutter. Cut the pieces in half vertically with the cutter.

3 — Slice one of the pieces in half to be used later for each of the two horizontal clasp connectors pictured above.

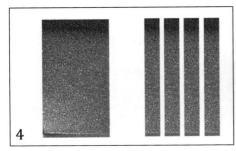

4 — Cut two non-textured pieces with the cutter then slice each vertically into fourths. You will need 8 for the finished bracelet.

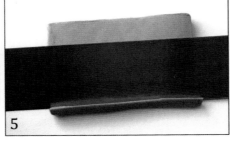

5 — Bevel the vertical backsides of all pieces by holding a tissue blade at a slight angle. Push into the clay.

6 — Set the beads face down on your surface. Place a half-inch craft stick in the center of the beads. Bring the edges loosely over the stick. Overlap and press the ends together.

SUPPLIES

Premo
Silver
Liquid polymer

Silver mica powder
Textured fabric
.50" black leather strap
Slide clasp

Black acrylic paint
.50" craft stick
E6000
1" x 1.50" cutter

7

With your finger, rub the textured pieces with silver mica powder.

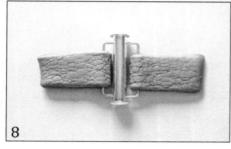

8

Thread the half-inch wide textured connectors into the ends of the clasps and press the clay ends together. Cure all the beads.

9

With a brush, apply a wash of black acrylic paint to the textured beads. Wipe the paint from the surface with a soft cloth.

10

Apply liquid polymer to the inside of two cured textured beads. Insert the clay clasp connectors half way into the bead and return them to the oven to bond.

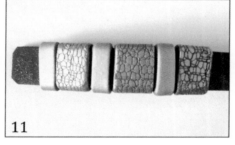

11

Cut the leather strap to measure 6.50" long. Slide the beads onto the strap alternating between textured and smooth beads.

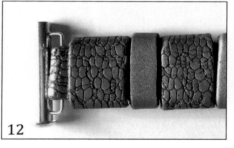

12

Apply E6000 to the inside of one clasp connector bead and insert the strap. Slide all the beads together. Glue the other clasp connector to the other end of the strap.

The Look of Snakeskin

Lace and other types of fabric can be used to create texture on clay. Look for loose, uneven weaves with interesting patterns like this fabric that impresses the clay with the look of snakeskin. Other woven items like spongy shelf liners or place mats can provide interesting designs.

Clay Slider

Clay • Extruded • Custom Fit

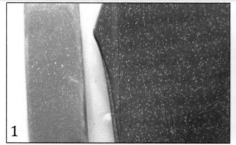

1

Mix a bit of red glitter clay to the blue a little at a time until a deep navy color is achieved.

Separately roll the three colors into logs with your hands. Load a 3/8" flat disk in the extruder along with one of the clay colors. You will need three strips of each color.

3

Stack one white strip on top of the other. Do the same with the red and blue leaving you with a total of three doubled strips of each color and three single strips of each color.

4

Drape the strips on a bracelet form. Wrap as many strips as will fit on the form. Cure the clay.

5

Only four clay thicknesses will fit in the clasp end so you will need to peel back ½" from the end of a white double strip with a craft knife and cut it off.

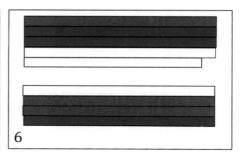

6

Create two stacks with the strips as shown here.

SUPPLIES

Premo
Red glitter
Blue glitter
White glitter

Jewelry glue
Clasp 10mm wide
Metal bracelet form
10mm metal star beads
Extruder

7

Hold the stacks together with masking tape.

8

Apply glue to the inside of the clasp and between all clay ends. Stuff them side-by-side into the clasp.

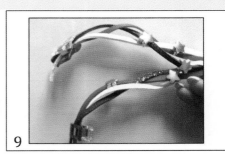

9

Slide two stars each onto the three doubled strips. Clip together the ends of the original left and right stacks. Loosely braid each.

10

Try on the bracelet and mark where to trim the clay to fit your wrist. Stack, glue, and stuff the ends into the clasp on the other side of the bracelet.

11

Slide the stars into the desired position. If some stars do not slide well, use a craft knife to shave off a bit of the strip.

12

If a star is too loose and does not stay in place, use a toothpick to slip glue inside the star to hold its position.

CORD

Stretchy Barrel Bead

Cord • Blended • 18mm Barrel Bead Form • Bracelet measures 7"

1

To create the barrel bead shapes, make a reusable form for them with the 18mm size Sculpey bead maker. See page 18 - "Easy Barrel Beads" for instructions. Eight beads were used for this project.

2

Blend equal amounts of all clay colors, then roll on the #5 setting.

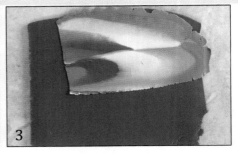

3

Roll solid Spanish olive for the bead base on the #1 setting. Set the blended clay strips on olive clay.

4

Cut beads to measure 1 1/8" x 1 1/4". Create a template the same size to mark holes in all four corners. With the medium Etch 'N Pearl tool, pierce holes in the clay.

5

Using a toothpick, line each hole with liquid polymer clay.

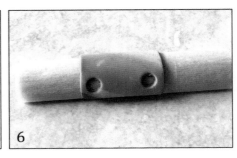

6

Cover the barrel form with parchment paper or aluminum foil. Drape the beads on the barrel.

SUPPLIES

Premo
Spanish Olive
Turquoise
Copper
White
Sculpey Bead Maker Tool

Etch 'N Pearl tool
Silver stretch cord
Eyelets
Aleene's Jewel-It

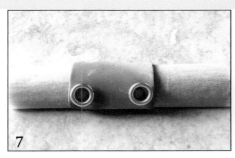

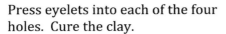

7

Press eyelets into each of the four holes. Cure the clay.

8

Sand and buff the beads. For more interest, allow the sander to take away a bit of the top layer in places so that the green layer underneath becomes visible.

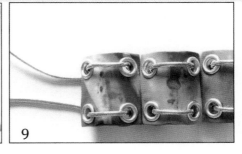

9

Cut two lengths of silver stretchy cord longer than the total number of beads. Weave the cord in and out of the eyelets with the cord on the outside.

10

Tie double knots in both cords on the inside of the bracelet and pull them very tight. Snip off excess cord. Coat the knot with Jewel-It or another flexible jewelry adhesive.

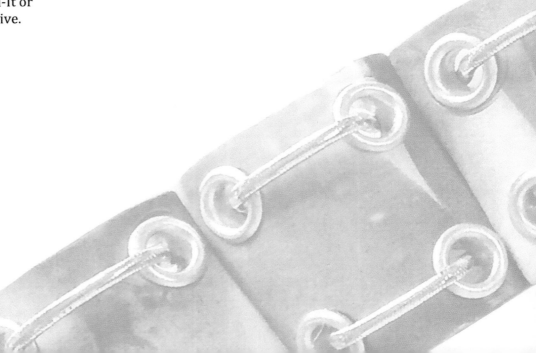

Celtic Multi Cord

Cord • Custom Template • Extruded • Bracelet Measures 8"

Create the texture sheet for the main piece by using the template on page 87. You will find complete instructions for turning the template into a texture sheet on page 12 and 13 - "Personalized Texture Sheets".

Mix a little burnt umber with the ecru. Roll the clay on the #1 setting. Press the texture sheet onto the clay and use a craft knife to cut the outline. With your finger, rub antique gold mica powder on the surface of the clay.

Create holes on both sides of the piece with a medium Etch 'N Pearl tool.

Place the piece on a bracelet blank to give it a slight curve. Attach clothespins to the blank to hold it upright in the oven.

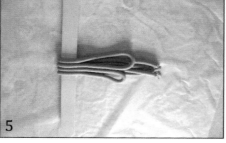

Use an extruder disc with five holes to create tubes for the four cord holders. Place four tubes on the work surface. Gently place a craft stick on the tubes. Wrap the tubes around the stick and blend the ends in the center. Rub the antique gold powder over the clay. Cure the cord holders and the focal piece.

Sand the edges of the focal piece. Brush a wash of black acrylic paint over the cured clay. Use a damp cloth to dab at the surface or wipe across the surface. Each technique will create a slightly different effect, but both will reveal the antique gold finish.

SUPPLIES

Premo
Burnt umber
Ecru
Liquid polymer
Etch 'N Pearl tool

Black acrylic clay
Craft stick
E6000
Magnetic clasp
Antique gold mica powder

Multi colored cotton cord
Krazy glue

Cut 24 eight-inch strands of the multi colored cord. Thread as many strands as you can into the needle and bring them through the side holes of the focal piece. Repeat until 15 are threaded on each side of the main clay piece.

Bring the strands through two cord holders on each side of the bracelet using the needle.

Even up the raw cord ends by cutting them to measure 2.50" long. Liberally apply adhesive to the strand ends and press them together.

Insert a craft stick all the way into the clasp opening. Mark the stick where the clasp ends. You will wrap the cord ends in the next step. Use the stick as a measure of how deep the wrap should be so it is not visible above the clasp.

Put a drop of crazy glue on the strands and press a 4" long piece of cord in the glue until it sets. Wrap the cord around the strands until the wrap is thick enough to fill the clasp hole and no deeper than the mark on the craft stick.

Apply more crazy glue and press down the end of the strand to secure it to the wrap. Cut off excess. Line the inside of the clasp pieces with glue and insert the wrapped ends.

Apply glue to the strands on the sides of the main piece and slide the cord holders over the glue.

Position the other two sliders between the glued ones and the clasp, and glue them in place.

Cord Stitch

Cord • Mokumé gané • Bracelet Measures 7.50"

1

Cut five solid purple 1.25" x 1.50" slices from clay rolled on the #1 setting. Wrap a 1.75" x 1.50" slice around the edges of a design block, then place the five slices on top. The block will hold the clay in place as you slice.

2

Using the mokumé gané technique, mist a design block with a desired texture and press it into the clay. Remove it and mist the blade of a potato peeler. Shave off seven thin layers of clay. Set them aside on paper.

3

Blend Purple and Ecru. Repeat the same technique used in step two with the solid purple, to cut seven thin, blended slices.

4

Set the blended slices on the paper with the purple pieces.

5

Use the cutter to create seven white rectangles rolled on the #3 setting.

6

Place a thin purple slice on each white one, followed by portions of a blended slice. Pull at the edges of the blended slices to create ragged edges to resemble frayed fabric.

SUPPLIES

Premo
Purple
White
Ecru
Liquid polymer
Sculpey design blocks

Hemp Cord
Krazy glue
Decorative spacer beads
Naihead wires

Card stock
Rectangular cutters
Wire cutters
Potato peeler

7 Cover the clay with baker's paper and cut the seven beads with a .75" x 1" rectangular cutter.

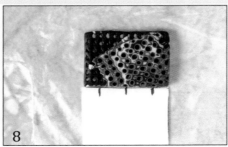

8 Create a card stock template with three corresponding holes on two edges of the paper. Space the holes evenly across the edge. Use the template to mark hole placement on the beads with an Etch 'N Pearl tool.

9 Trim a nailhead wire to .25". Dip the wire stem into liquid polymer and slip it through a small decorative spacer bead.

10 Press wires into different areas of each of the seven beads. Cure the beads.

11 Cut nine 4" pieces of cord. Connect two beads by moving the cord through the holes and crossing in the front. At the bottom, tie a double knot in the cord on the wrong side. Connect all the remaining beads with the cord.

12 Attach the clasps by winding the cord around the clasp end and moving through the holes on the end beads. Tie a double knot on the back side.

13 Apply Jewel-It glue to the knots. When the glue is dry, cut off all the excess cord.

MAGNETS

Top Mount Magnet Bangle

Magnet • Skinner Blend/Cane • 1.50" Bracelet form

1

Create two skinner blends; one with
periwinkle and white and one with periwinkle and rose gold.

2

Use the blends to make two bullseye canes with a white tube at the end of the rose gold clay and a gold tube on the white end of the other clay. Push against the tubes to roll each strip into cylinders.

3

Separately, roll gold and white clay on the #4 setting to create outer wraps for the cylinders. Place the gold wrap around the cylinder with the gold center. Place the white wrap around the one with the white center.

4

Cut thin slices from each cylinder. Flatten one side and pinch the other to create a teardrop shape. Curl one skinny edge over another to form petals.

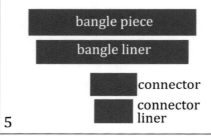

bangle piece

bangle liner

connector

connector liner

5

Cut three 8" x 1.50" wide pieces of periwinkle rolled on the #2 setting. From the pieces, cut the main bangle first to fit completely around your bracelet form minus one inch. The bangle liner piece should be 1" shorter than the bangle. Cut the connector next to measure 1.50". The connector liner should measure .75".

6

Wrap the bangle and its liner on the form with the shorter liner layer on top. Position it .50" away from the ends of the bangle layer.

The Top Mount Magnet Bangle is no ordinary bracelet. The rose gold petals jut out, sparkling and circling the wrist in a flamboyant fashion, making a strong artistic statement.

SUPPLIES

Premo
Periwinkle blue
White
Rose Gold
Liquid polymer

.25" Neodymium magnets
marker

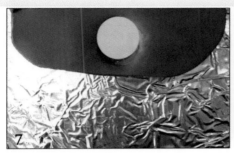
7

8

9

Push magnets into the bangle layer's margin. Remove them and apply liquid polymer to the sunken clay. Match two magnet pieces, then pull them apart and mark the sides that grip to avoid mismatched pieces after curing.

Replace the marked magnets into the clay. Position petals on the bangle clay, clearing the 1/2" margins at the front opening. Arrange the petals on the connector so they fit in with the ones on the bangle.

Roll scraps of clay into balls on the work surface. Press them into the spaces between the petal stems. Cure the clay.

10

11

12

Place the connector onto the cured bangle on the form matching the seams. Press the clay onto the magnet to create an impression. Remove the raw clay, then the cured clay from the form.

Apply liquid polymer to the recesses for the connector magnets and insert them on the underside. Place the piece on the form to shape it.

Attach petals and balls as you did for the bangle. Cure the connector.

13

Remove the connector from the form. Sand rough edges on both the connector and the bangle. To wear, slip your wrist into the bracelet. Match up the magnets on the connector and the bangle to close the bracelet.

Open Bangle

Bangle With Connector

Side Mount Magnet Bangle

Magnet • Sutton Slice • Blended • 18mm tube form

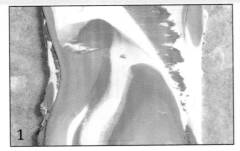

1. On the work surface roll out tubes of blue, wasabi, and white clay. Sheet the clay on the #1 setting.

2. Use the Sutton Slice technique of pressing chunks of clay into the rubber stamp. Fill all the crevices. As you fill the stamp, use a tissue blade to shave the surface with the intent of removing all but the filled areas.

3. When you are done, the raised rubber surface image should be clean.

4. Turn the stamp over and press it onto a black piece of clay rolled on the #1 setting, measuring 5.75" x 2.25".

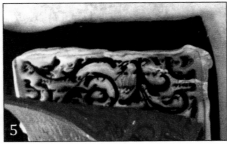

5. Slowly peel the rubber stamp off the clay. If some of the color clay lifts in the process, just press it back down and it will adhere. Remove the entire stamp. Follow steps one through five to create another identical textured clay piece.

6. Roll new black clay into two tubes thick enough to fill two 18mm bead forms. Mist the forms before adding clay. Once filled, trim the ends straight with a blade. Imprint a texture into the flat clay bottom if desired. It will be on the inside of the bracelet and add a unique touch. Remove the clay from the forms.

SUPPLIES

Premo
Blue
Wasabi
Black
White
Sculpey Bead Maker forms 18mm
Liquid polymer

Rubber stamp
Power drill
E6000
Tape
Parchment paper

.25" Neodymium magnets

Join the tubes to create one long piece. Cover it with the Sutton Slice which will need to be pieced together to achieve the right length. Turn the covered tube on its side and trim the color ends flush with the black clay.

Wrap the tube completely around a bracelet form with the two ends touching. Use a tissue blade to slice through the clay and remove a two inch section. Set it aside.

Wrap parchment paper loosely around the bangle clay to hold it in place while curing on the form. Secure the paper with tape. Cure the bangle.

Cure the two inch section on the bracelet form. When cool, check the alignment of the bangle and the small section. If there are slight spaces between the bangle ends and the small section ends, roll a thin tube of black clay and press it to the bangle ends and cure.

Mark the centers of the two ends of the bangle and the small section. Drill holes large and deep enough in each to accommodate the magnets. Apply E6000 to each hole and press in a magnet. To wear the bracelet, slip the open bangle on your wrist then fill the opening with the small section. The two parts will pop together seamlessly.

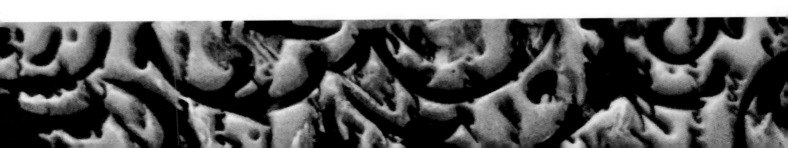

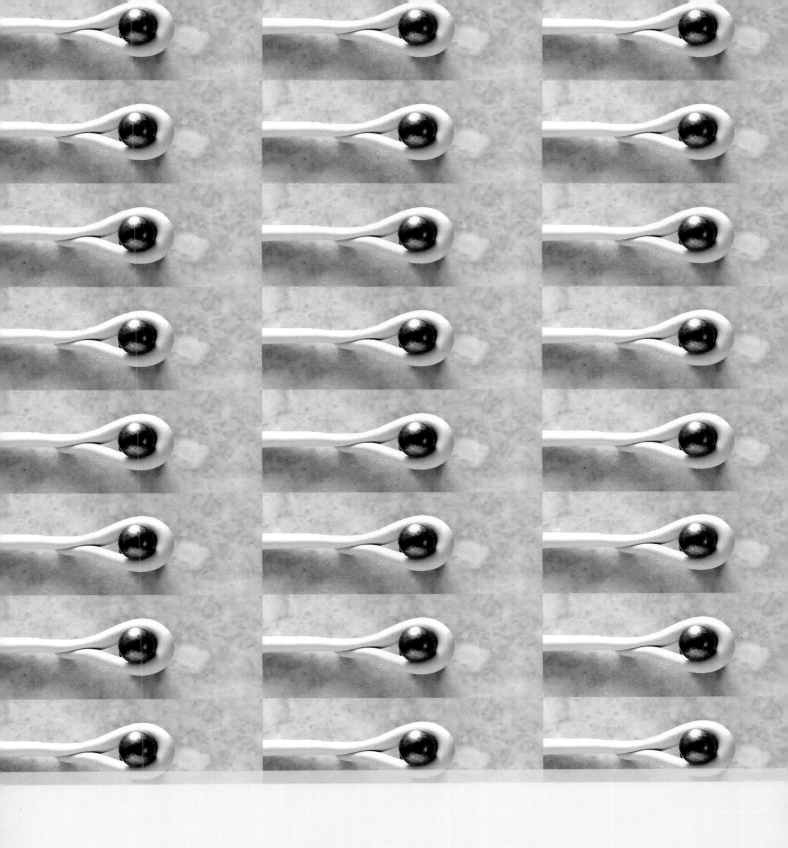

HOOKS & LOOPS & SNAPS

Hook Cuff

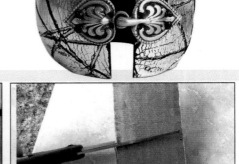

Cord Wrap Texture • Metal Leaf • 2" Bracelet Form

Roll a piece of black clay approximately 2" x 9" on the #1 setting. Rub a sheet of silver leaf onto the clay. Follow package directions.

Place the clay on bakers paper cut to just slightly larger than the clay.

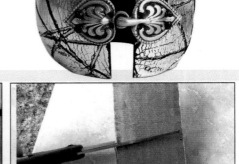

Cut a stiff piece of cardboard 1/2" bigger all around than the clay. Snip little slits on all the edges.

Place the clay and paper on the cardboard.

Tie a knot in a strand of cotton cord. Slip it into a cardboard slit to secure it. Wrap the cord over the clay and into the slits. Work in random patterns from side to side, vertically, and at angles.

When you are happy with the pattern, pass an acrylic roller over the the clay, pressing the cord into the clay to create impressions.

SUPPLIES

Premo
Black
Liquid polymer
Etch 'N Pearl tool

Cotton cord
Clasp
Cardboard
Scissors
Silver leaf

7

Carefully remove the cord from the clay. Remove the clay from the plastic.

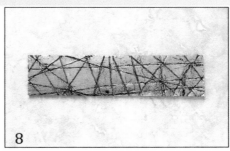

8

Cut the piece to measure 2" wide and the desired length to fit your bangle form. See instructions on page 15 for creating "Custom Bracelet Forms". Wrap the clay around the form cupping the sides to curve the piece.

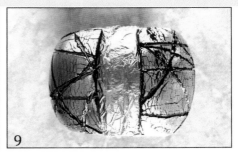

9

Slice a straight .75" section out of one end of the clay.

10

Apply liquid polymer to the backside of the clasp pieces and center them on the clay ends.

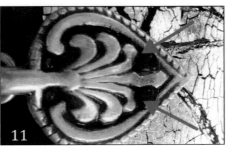

11

Use the smallest Etch 'N Pearl tool to create tiny black dots to cover the two holes on each clasp piece. Be sure the clay comes in contact with the liquid polymer. Cure the clay.

12

Remove the clay from the form. Sand rough edges, avoiding silver leaf. Protect the bracelet finish with a glaze.

Hardware Loop Wrap

Loop Wrap • Texture Sheet • 2" Bracelet Form

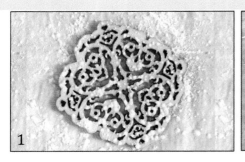

Mix equal parts ecru and white. Roll out the blend on the #1 setting. The clay piece should measure 8.50" x 1.50". Rub baby powder on the die cut wood.

Impress the wood image on the clay starting on one end.

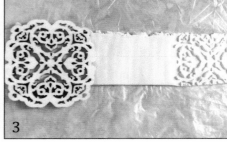

Measure down 8.50" and impress that end. Press a third time to create the design in the center of the clay strip.

Cut curves in the short edges of the clay strip to match the wood edge design.

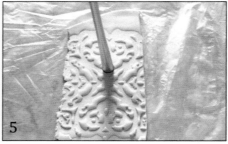

Make a hole with a medium Etch 'N Pearl tool centered 1.25" from one end of the clay. If you need a longer bracelet, move the hole closer to the edge.

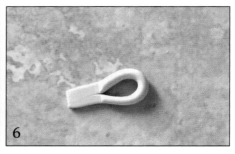

On the work surface, roll a thin piece of matching clay into a tube. Create a loop for the end of the bracelet. Press the ends together

SUPPLIES

Premo
Ecru
White
Etch 'N Pearl tool

Tim Holtz hardware
Die cut wood
Baby powder
Blue, copper, silver mica powder

7

Attach the loop to the clay end opposite the hole. Be sure the loop opening will fit around the hardware before attaching it.

8

Apply mica powder in blue, copper, and silver on raised areas as desired.

9

Cover the colored clay loosely with bakers paper.

10

Use the paper to help wrap the clay and shape it to the glass form without smudging the powder.

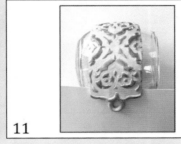

11

Once the clay is in place, remove the bakers paper. Insert a piece of card stock between overlapping clay ends to keep them from baking together during curing. Cure the clay.

12

Install the two-piece hardware into the open hole. Push the screw into the wrong side of the clay and twist the knob on from the right side. Glaze the project to protect the mica powder finish.

Leather Snap Strap

Snap • Template • Gold Foil • 1.50" Bracelet Form   *bracelet measures 1 3/8" wide at the center*

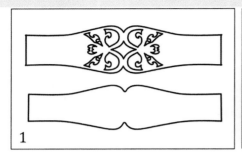

1

Import the templates into your stencil cutting machine. You will find them on page 87. Trace them to create a cut file. See the complete instructions for blade settings and cutting clay on a stencil machine on page 21.

2

Roll the clay on your pasta machine on a #5 setting. Position the clay on freezer paper and send it to cut. Remove the cut pieces.

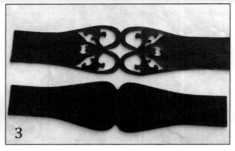

3

Roll out another piece of clay to cut the liner using the second template. The liner is a bit smaller and does not contain the cuts in the center.

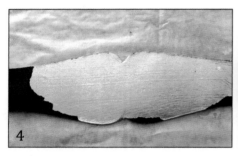

4

Rub gold foil on the center of the liner. The top cut clay piece will allow the gold to show through.

5

Apply liquid polymer to the back side of the fancy cut clay. Stack the two bracelet layers and press together.

6

Apply liquid polymer to the leather strap edge.

SUPPLIES

Premo
Black
Etch 'N Pearl tool
Liquid polymer

Gold foil
Leather snap pieces
Freezer paper
Silhouette stencil cutting machine

Place the leather glue side down on the strap front. Use the Etch 'N Pearl tool to cut small round pieces to cover the holes in the leather. Be sure the clay comes in contact with the liquid polymer. Stuff scraps of clay in the holes if necessary.

Wrap the bracelet around your bracelet form. Cure.

Cutting This Project with a Craft Knife

This bracelet design does not require a stencil cutting machine. It can be cut with a craft knife if you have the patience to work with the tiny details. If you choose to use a knife, print out the templates on card stock. Cut them out and transfer the design onto the clay.

Follow the instructions starting with step #3 to complete the project.

Cutting Clay On A Stencil Machine

Cutting clay on a stencil machine requires that it be very thin. That might sound limiting for some projects, but it does have advantages. Two thin clay pieces can be joined together for a thicker bracelet and the two can produce a much more flexible result. This strap bracelet is a good example. It is made of two layers rolled on the #5 setting of the pasta machine. It flexes as any thin leather strap might. It's also more comfortable than most thicker clay bracelets.

You would not want to use a stencil machine for cutting all your clay, but it certainly is another useful tool to have in your polymer clay arsenal.

Printable Templates & Stencils

Wired Under The Sea page 26

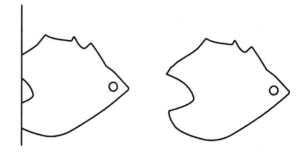

Coiled Wire Cane page 28

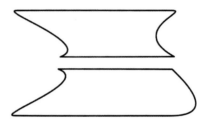

Custom Birds On A Wire page 52

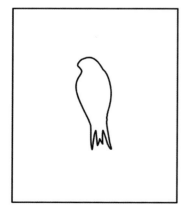

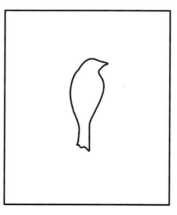

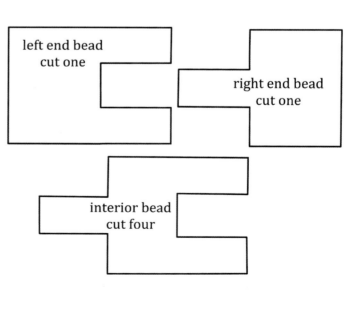

left end bead
cut one

right end bead
cut one

interior bead
cut four

Printable Templates & Stencils

Tab Hinge page 56

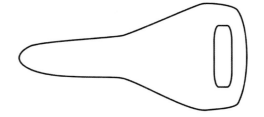

Celtic Multi Cord page 68

Leather Snap Strap page 84

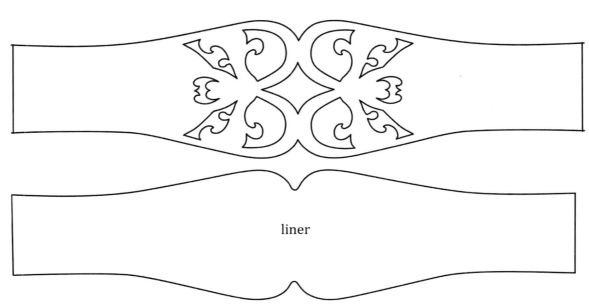

liner

About the Author

Gloria Uhler is a career writer and designer with interests in an eclectic range of topics. Her accomplishments include a produced feature film, and numerous articles in print as well as online.

A full fledged clay addict, Gloria shares many of her craft creations through free tutorials on her website www.domestic-divaonline.com. She also creates craft tutorials for hire. Her projects have appeared in *Craft Ideas Magazine*, *Altered Couture* and other craft publications.

Gloria lives in Southern California.

Contact her at domestic-diva@cox.net
Follow Divaonline1 on Twitter
Follow Gloria Guy on Facebook

NOTE

Every effort has been made to provide valid sources for the tools and supplies used in this book. Please bear in mind, information can easily become obsolete as vendors discontinue products.

When "store" is used in the reference, the items were purchased at my local store and may not be available at that company's website.

DREMEL
dremel.com
rotary tool

eBay
ebay.com
search for item ID#
221558438787
hinge pg. 38

FIRE MOUNTAIN GEMS
firemountaingems.com
bracelet clasps pg. 34, 40, 42, 54, 56, 60, 70

FOX RUN BRANDS
foxbrands.com
Cookie Cutter Rectangles

HOBBY LOBBY STORE
hobbylobby.com
Woodpile Hinges pg. 40
Metal Gallery star beads pg. 62
Silver stretch cord pg. 66
Magnetic clasp pg. 68

JAN'S JEWELRY SUPPLY
jansjewels.com
Spring hinge pg. 46
Spring hinge pg. 48
Brass bracelet pg. 50

JOANN STORE
joann.com
End caps pg. 32
Copper clasp pg. 48
Hook hardware pg. 80
Blue Moon leather snaps pg. 84

LOWE'S
Texture tool pg. 54

MICHAELS STORE
michaels.com
Clasp pg. 24
Clasp pg. 28
End caps pg. 38
Bead Landing clasp pg. 62
Bead Landing cord pg. 68 & 70
Wood die cuts pg. 82
All Wire, Jump rings, & Chain

MINIHANDS
etsy.com
Hinges pg. 42

MONA LISA PRODUCTS
speedballart.com
Silver & gold leaf foils pg. 40, 80, 84

POLYFORM PRODUCTS
sculpey.com
Beadmaker tool pg. 18
Cabochon molds pg. 24
Design block pg. 19
Eyelets pg. 66
Comb tool pg. 26
Multiple projects: Premo clay, Etch 'N pearl tool, Liquid polymer, Super slicer blades, Acrylic roller, Comb tool.

PROMAG
promagproducts.com
.25" X 6.3mm Magnets

RANGER
rangerink.com
Mica powder pg. 48, 52, 54, 58, 60, 68, 82

SPECTRUM NOIR
spectrumnoir.com
Alcohol pens pg. 42

SILHOUETTE AMERICA
silhouetteamerica.com
Cameo stencil cutting machine pg. 20

TIM HOLTZ
timholtz.com
Watch hardware pg. 58
Ball fastener pg. 82

WALNUT HOLLOW
walnuthollow.com
Extruder

Free Clay Jewelry Tutorials Online

at www.Domestic-Divaonline.com

14938308R10051

Printed in Great Britain
by Amazon.co.uk, Ltd.,
Marston Gate.